COMING TO NOTHING
AND FINDING EVERYTHING

D1366620

COMING TO NOTHING AND FINDING EVERYTHING

PRISON, THE HEADLESS WAY, AND THE MAN IN THE OTHER BATHROOM

By J.C. Amberchele

COMING TO NOTHING AND FINDING EVERYTHING

ISBN: 978-1-7926624-6-1

Cover art "Shadow Walking" by Oscar Senn

A slightly different version of "Patch of Green" first appeared in the magazine New Age Journal in 1985.

"The Time of Your Life" was published in the Winter 2000 issue of Turning Wheel.

"Impromptu Awakening" and "No-Mindfulness" appeared in the 1999 Fall and 2001 Spring/Summer issues respectively of Inner Directions Journal.

Also by J.C. Amberchele:

The Light That I Am
The Almighty Mackerel and His Holy Bootstraps
The Heavenly Backflip
Cracked Open
How You Lose (A novel in stories)

In the beginning . . .

God meets Himself and discovers He has nothing to do because He is already Everything That Is, for which He is grateful, of course, even though He doesn't know why or even what this "Everything" is that He is, or why He is awake to this fact and appears to be Here/Now, despite the fact that He sees there is no separate one to be or not be anywhere or anywhen.

Look within!
The secret is inside you."
—Hui-Neng

"We have two eyes to see two sides of things, but there must be a third eye which will see everything at the same time and yet not see anything. That is to understand Zen."
—D.T. Suzuki

"What you are looking for is where you are looking from."
—St. Francis of Assisi

"What we truly are is God manifest in time and place.
Know this and live well until you die."
—Rabbi Rami Shapiro

"The fact is that you are not the body.
The Self does not move but the world moves in it."
—Ramana Maharshi

"Look here and know who you are.
Instantly you will find freedom, and this Suffering—hitchhiking from womb to womb—will Instantly stop. The only way is to look within."
—Sri H.W.L. Poonja

"Suddenly and abruptly I recognized myself."
—Meng Shan

"What a universe it is, what incredible richness And variety gush tirelessly
From this unutterably simple I AM THAT I AM."
—D.E. Harding

Table of Contents

FOREWORD

I've had the pleasure of knowing and walking alongside Amberchele for many years. His life story is dramatic, a descent into the Underworld if ever there was one followed by a breakthrough into 'country of everlasting clearness.' In this book he tells us stories from his journey, including the time he was in a Mexican jail—and how he escaped!—as well as tales from his long incarceration in a U.S. prison. How different his path has been from mine. And yet, in some ways, not so different.

Amberchele writes with honesty, humility and humour, painting with vivid word-pictures his adventures. But what also enables me to enter deeply into his mind and heart is his direct seeing and valuing of the Self at the core of himself, the one who is 'the soul of my soul.' Again and again he brings onto the front burner This which is most clear and most dear to him—This which is visible to anyone who looks. As he describes his view from his Single Eye, I am right there with him, nearer to him than he is to himself. If like Amberchele you are drawn to the One, fascinated by the One, in love with the One, then I think you'll find in him a friend.

So often what the Self pulls out of the magic hat of itself is unpredictable, in both small ways and big. A dramatic illustration of this comes when Amberchele's life takes a new direction. A radically new direction. Suddenly, after 35 years in prison, in his late seventies, in not great health, with little money and only the clothes on his back, he is released . . .

But, as he says, if you can't trust This, what can you trust?

When we turn our attention round from what we are looking at to what we are looking out of, we see that each of us is the One. And importantly, each of us is also a unique life lived by the One, a special expression of the One. This book invites you to feel your way into another of the One's lives. Take this opportunity to see what it's like being the One from Amberchele's point of view. You will be enriched by the experience.

Richard Lang, December 2018

INTRODUCTION

In Buddhism, it is said that when the Buddha became enlightened, all beings were enlightened, for when the Buddha became enlightened, he saw that all beings were inside him, and thus were him.

This is the overall theme of this book, from the early articles in Part I that were written from within the prison experience, through the period of sudden realization and cumulative understanding in Part II, and on to the joy of universal acceptance in Part III. It is not a book about Buddhism or any other ism. It is more a conversation about Who We Really Are, which ultimately is a conversation with ourSelf.

A few of the chapters in this book appeared as magazine articles; others were never published. The chapter entitled "Leaf" in Part I is fiction, while the remainder of that section and all of the chapters in Parts II and III are non-fiction. Each, whether written during the first decade of my prison sentence or included more recently, arrived unbidden, either penciled on note paper or typed on a portable or eventually keyed into this old laptop, appearing in and as this mysterious and awake No-thing.

Special thanks to Richard Lang, coordinator of the Shollond Trust and The Headless Way, for consistently pointing to awakening and showing so many others the same. Also to Douglas and Catherine Harding, who demonstrated that I am not what others say I am, based on what I look like from where they are. I am, rather, exactly what I see for myself when I turn my attention around and look within.

You are invited to do the same, and to that end, Douglas and friends have invented several simple but powerful "experiments," many of which can be found in my earlier work The Light That I Am, or in several of Harding's and Richard Lang's books. As a result, one look in the right direction may be the world shaking, world-ending event it was for me, or it may not. Suffice it to say that it requires a look, not a read, but should a word in this book at least point to the "gateless gate" of awakening, then the Beatific Vision is surely to follow.

PART ONE

PRISON

"Why do you stay in prison
when the door is so wide open?"
—Rumi

A PATCH OF GREEN

I have sixteen years of lower and higher education to my credit, along with a Bachelor of Arts degree. Not a remarkable feat these days, but the education was good: a private Quaker school in Philadelphia, a fine suburban high school in New Jersey where we "preppies" wore white bucks and rode our Raleighs to class, two years at a small liberal arts college in Pennsylvania, and a dean's list graduation from a university in New York. Splendid preparation for the position I've been holding—assistant janitor of Pod C-1 in this far-removed state penitentiary. Pay: $1.12 per week.

Today, however, I have spiraled to an all-time low. I am now assistant laundryman as well, which is about as far down the unholy ladder as one can get. To carry out this task I remove the trash from a large plastic barrel, foist the barrel into the shower stall, and fill it with hot water (if there is any), cheap soap powder, and the nastiest conglomeration of soiled clothes this side of San Quentin. The wash and rinse cycles are accomplished with the help of a makeshift plunger, the product of an unlikely marriage of plastic soup bowl and broomstick; "spin dry" means wet blisters on the palms of my hands from wringing countless pairs of state socks and underwear. The final result is a dripping gray mass hanging from the metal railings of the second tier like seaweed draped from the gunnels of a rusting ship. There should be a better way to do this here, but no one has invented it yet.

This is a maximum-security prison. Should the bars come unglued, the public would have something to be concerned about, what with more than three hundred terminally bored convicts running amok in an already crime-ridden society full of terrified law-abiding citizens. But life in prison is not the minute-by-minute horror story one is led to believe. There are some pretty nice folks here, at least folks who were probably pretty nice before they arrived.

There are, of course, a few strange ones — inmates who tread the high-wire of separate realities, faltering with every step. Mustard Bob, bless his heart, puts mustard on his pudding and Jell-O in his taco shells. Mumblin' Phil has twenty-four-hour nightmares and wards off imaginary monsters by jamming cigarettes up his nose. Maybe he knows why. Then there are the slugs — hopeless inmates in dull green uniforms — those referred to by the guards as "good for nothing." Too burdened with negative conditioning to step in either direction, they are buffeted about like dust balls on the prison floor, passed down the institutional line, and eventually swept out onto the street where they may or may not make it. And finally, there are the habitually violent, men who rarely emerge from the special cages they are housed in, and then only in chains. Shocking people with shocking crimes, they are the most distressing, as much because they are a danger to society as because they are part of us all, the toxic waste of a culture that cares too often for the wrong things for the wrong reasons.

Today I am standing by one of the two pod windows made of multiple slabs of what appears to be sledgehammer-resistant glass. The view looks onto a long and empty asphalt mall surrounded by cellblocks and work units, and dominated on the western end by the administration building. The tower, not unlike those used for traffic control at major airports, looms menacingly above the mall, a bastion of security for the staff and a warning to us. The entire complex is constructed of unpainted cement blocks, resembling a munitions bunker in the Nevada desert.

But in the middle of this anomaly, adjacent to the

administration building and in front of my window, there is a tiny patch of perfectly green lawn, punctuated at both ends by flowers — tulips, daffodils, and geraniums. A convict tends it with loving care. The administrators have put their mark on it by bordering it with railroad ties, military style, and clipping its grass rigidly short to match their flattop haircuts. It is as if they placed it here as a final word, a reminder of our obedience to the groomed oppression of their system.

I am standing here in front of this window in front of this lawn, surrounded by this mess I've gotten myself into for the rest of my life — smiling. It is a gesture as close to tears as to laughter. A friend approaches, and I can tell that he is worried that I see something he doesn't, or worse, that I have joined the ranks of those who won't make it. If he should ask why I am smiling, I'll have to tell him the thought that just crossed my mind, but I know he won't feel the nameless emotion that is out of proportion to the words, or smell the sweet musk of earth and grass, or hear me scream louder than I could with my voice, but I'll tell him anyway, quietly:

It's the lawn. No matter how any times they clip it, it keeps growing back.

THE TIME OF YOUR LIFE

Before I came to prison I saw time as linear, racing or dragging but nevertheless advancing reliably into a future of personal advantage, often at the cost of others. But prison changed that. To be sent to prison is to be cut off, removed, sealed in a void. Gone were family and friends, gone the comfortable routine of my job, gone also the weekends in the mountains, gone even my clothes, my watch, my hair. To be in prison is to go nowhere, not in the sense of treading water but of drowning repeatedly, and in this it is relentless: the boredom, the fear, the violence are constant reminders. But above all, to come to prison is to stop abruptly: to a new prisoner the world literally quits, and what remains seems endlessly empty, without dimension.

When I first arrived, I experienced the most profound sense of absence, a feeling I never could have imagined before. This same knowledge of timelessness, I have heard, is experienced by people who choose suicide: a past too painful to remember, a future that appears hopeless at best, and the unbearable present of life in prison.

But slowly, perhaps to prevent myself from going insane, I built a life inside these walls. I found a job, friends, time to write. For many prisoners it is easier to pick up where they left off, reestablishing the habits that brought them here in the first place. The tiers are crowded with con men and thieves, gangsters and thugs. But for some, the shock of prison is so great that it propels them in a new direction.

Not long after I arrived I met a man doing "life" on a major drug charge. Despite the time he was facing, he filled his days with good cheer and positive effort. This man—with twenty years to parole eligibility— was a fervent member of AA and of academic and church groups. Although he earned no more than $1.50 a day at his job, he was perhaps more dedicated than the entire hierarchy of staff supervisors above him. One day I asked him why he was so enthusiastic.

"Why not?" he replied.

And I believe this is when I began to view time differently. "Why not?" became for me—not suddenly but with the sort of shift in thinking that requires months or years—a source of inner strength, a catchphrase for personal motivation. "Why not?" became "Sure—why not!"

Not long ago my son and daughter came to visit me. My daughter had done some research on our family tree and brought news that her grandfather, my father, whom I had not seen nor spoken to in nearly 20 years, had died of a heart attack the year following my arrest. Hardly remembering him herself, having met him only once when she was young, she patted my arm and waited for my reaction. When none came, she took my hand and continued talking about her new job and new apartment, eventually passing the conversation over to my son, who had much to say about his high school football team.

For the rest of the visit I listened, laughed at their stories, and felt their excitement and hope for the future, but it was not easy. I kept thinking about my dad, and about time, doing time, and what it has meant for me. I had missed more than a decade of my children's lives, nearly their entire teenage years, and would miss countless more. I had missed my father's funeral without even knowing he had died, and worse, I had missed the opportunity to tell him at least once that I loved him.

But I was also thinking that, if nothing else, prison, with its rigid conformity and structured regularity, has taught me that time is cyclical, not linear. I see time now as a great spiral, corkscrewing out of the past and carrying with it all the complex moments of history, and always coming around, coming around. The world, I have realized, allows for second chances, but only if you create them. And it is not enough to make room for new habits among the old ones; second chances are created from within, in a process that either begins with a change of attitude or begins not at all, a process that requires altering a lifetime of familiar but self-defeating beliefs. Why not?

Years ago when I was in college, my father unexpectedly appeared at my Homecoming Day football game. I played defense on the team, and during the first period of a game we were already losing, there he was, on the sideline near the end zone in his topcoat and Stetson. I intercepted a pass that day, and our team made a spectacular comeback in the fourth quarter to win, but even more amazing was that my dad had driven 300 miles to attend that game. Afterwards, in the locker room, because we didn't know what to say to each other, because we never knew what to say, I told him I had a date, and he left for home, 300 miles in an empty car.

There is no changing the past—I had told myself this a thousand times, especially in the years after coming to prison. But time as a spiral transcends linear time, and yet contains it. And so there are moments—a thought, a touch, a way of seeing the world—that radiate from the present not only to the future but to the past as well.

Near the end of the Sunday visiting hours, inmates and visitors are separated and herded to opposite areas, the visitors into a sally port for exiting and the inmates to a hallway where they are strip searched. Just before this, in the act of parting, inmates and visitors are permitted to hug and kiss briefly.

We stood, my son and daughter and I. My thought was that my daughter had never found it difficult to express her feelings or show affection in these situations, but I was not sure how my son would react. Before this day, I had not seen him in nearly a decade, not since he was eight years old, and all through the visit I kept thinking how much he looked and acted like me, and therefore how much he looked and acted like my father. And so we stood and faced each other, and there were no tears in my son's eyes nor in mine, and it was obvious that neither of us knew what to do with our hands . . . but then all three of us embraced, and suddenly it was so natural and easy for me to say how much I love him, how much I love them both. In that time-full moment, it occurred to me that my father was listening, that he had heard every word as clearly as though he were present.

FREEDOM

"Only so long as chains remain uninspected are they altogether binding, for freedom is the inescapable condition of self-consciousness."
—*Douglas Harding*

One thing I've noticed all these years is that prisoners like to talk about the conditions in other prisons, as if by this comparison they might improve their mood or gain yet another reason to voice a complaint. I often hear about the available canteen items in faraway states such as Illinois or Georgia, or which facility has the worst cells and how many men are forced to live in them, where the best jobs are or how late the yard is open on summer nights in Oregon or Minnesota.

So when someone asks if I've done time before, and I answer that I once did a stretch in a Mexican prison, invariably they exclaim, "Oh man! What was that like?"

I have a stock answer: "Just like the film Midnight Express," and I might also mention the bust by the *Federales*, the beatings and threats, the Napoleonic law that meant I was guilty until proven innocent. But this rarely suffices; almost always they want to know more about the conditions, what it was really like to live in a Mexican prison.

So I tell them about the stone walls and the ancient gun towers and how the cellblocks were Quonset style—a hundred men in each of those sweltering buildings with nothing more than a hole in the cement for a toilet, a pipe with running water for a shower.

And no cells. Instead, there were indoor shantytowns, cardboard and plywood shacks similar to those on the hills in Rio or behind the landfills in Mexico City, except miniaturized and crammed together into long rows. In the aisles between, the "buffaloes" roamed, the down-and-out who couldn't afford the price of a shack, who paced all day and slept at night wherever they stopped.

There was no yard to speak of, only a cement patio called a "loma" fronting the cellblocks, so crowded at times that one could scarcely move. No gym, no weight pile, no track or ball fields, and one telephone for nearly a thousand men, an old metal hotel phone with no dial, incoming calls only. Should a man's luck run out—the dreaded medical emergency—there was a small clinic in a room above the ad-seg building, with a half-dozen beds and one nurse. Once, a group of well-meaning nuns brought cauldrons of chicken mole to feed the entire population; everyone was sick for days, with long lines at both the clinic and the toilet holes. The nurse left, overwhelmed.

It was the stink of the place that got to me the most. The noise—the nearly continuous shouting, clanging, hammering, the din of tinny ranchero music blaring from dozens of portable radios—became oddly tolerable over time, likely because there was a semblance of peace each night after ten o'clock. But the stench, like the bedbugs, assaulted me all the more at night. Especially noxious was the shithole on evenings when it had rained and the sewer line had backed up; that, and the forty or fifty "buffaloes" sprawled in the aisle in their filthy clothing created a smell that more than once drove me to bury my face in my pillow in an effort to fall asleep.

When money arrived, my fall-partner and I built a plywood shack on stilts, above the fray. We installed a swamp cooler, built wooden bunks, bought a TV and a stereo and an ice cooler for the occasional beer we could score from the guards. We hired a cook and a laundry man and paid a trustee to run errands between cellblocks during lock-up.

For if a man had money, this was a prison like no other, at least not in the States. Everything from tacos to toilet paper was sold at the prison store; for anything else, there were kids with bikes outside the front gate who would shop at the local *mercado* or any restaurant in town. A man could buy food, clothing, lumber, art supplies, appliances, drugs, booze, even prostitutes, for the right price.

But I soon learned that none of this worked for me. Nothing, no amount of temporary comfort, nothing I could buy or surround myself with could change the loathing I felt. I wanted out. I was obsessed with escape. It wasn't that I was afraid for my life, for even there, a man who did his time and no one else's was usually left alone. And I had a short sentence: only five years, less than four, with good-time. But I couldn't stay a month, a week, an hour longer—for me, every minute in that hell-hole was worse than the beating suffered at the hands of the *Federales*.

I went on a diet and lost forty pounds so I could fit in a trash barrel, hoping to be carted out with the garbage, but the plan fell through. I paid the guards to take me to a dentist downtown, arranged for a friend to kidnap me, but the friend never showed. I faked a fall in the cellblock and spent three weeks crapping on newspaper shut away in my stilt-house, pretending I couldn't walk. When the guards finally took me to a hospital, it was the wrong one. I had paid two thousand dollars to a man who claimed his brother was a doctor at a hospital where I was surely to be taken; from there I was to be hustled to a rear exit and a waiting car, it was all arranged. All along I half knew it was a setup, that I was the mark, but what did I care?—even the slimmest of chances brought hope.

So I planned a tunnel, smuggling in a drill and moving from

the stilt-house to a better location in another cellblock with other Americans, four of us constructing false walls and ceilings in our shacks to hold dirt and rocks, and in one room, a trick bed that when disassembled exposed the work area beneath it. Months passed, drilling that foot-thick cement floor, worried sick that the noise would alert the guards or other inmates who would tell on us.

For we knew about the water-hole, a five-by-five concrete box with only one barred window near the ceiling; the guards would drop a man in via a trap door on the roof and fill it up to his neck with water. A man could spend days in there, hanging on the bars of that window, sleepless, shitting and pissing in the water, watching the bugs float past his chin.

And then one day not eighteen months into my sentence I walked out of that place and got into a car and left for the U.S., as simple as that. A wealthy Mexican drug lord, a convict with as much power as the warden but who couldn't escape because his family lived in town, brought me to his luxury cell and dressed me in a suit, fitted me with a wig and remade my face with tanning cream and a phony mustache, then handed me a briefcase and sent me out the front gate as his visiting attorney, right past the guards. And it didn't cost a dime. He wanted me to wholesale his pot in the States, and I did that for a while, but it was low-grade and hard to sell, so I moved on to better deals.

And so my prison experience in Mexico was over, less than two years after it had begun. My partner was still there, however, still drilling tiny holes in that square of cement under the bed. He broke through, eventually, and little by little over the next six months he and the others managed to dig a narrow tunnel nearly a hundred feet under two walls to the street. I was there with a crew and a van when they came out on a Sunday morning, and the exhilaration was every bit as intense as the day I'd left via the front door.

Today, I no longer think about escape. After years in a U.S. prison, the rush is long gone. Men ask me why I had risked my life back then, or why I was so crazy as to return for my partner — were the conditions really that bad? I guess I once thought they were. But then one day years later I got to thinking that, in Mexico at least, I had conjugal visits: every Thursday my wife could stay five hours in my shack, while those with no visit had to leave the cellblock and remain on the *loma*. And there, at least, I could wear my own clothes, cook what I wanted, move freely throughout the prison without the humiliation of pat-searches and strip-outs, carry money and ID in my own wallet. There were rules but not petty rules; there was not the daily threat of a write-up for a minor infraction such as an extra sheet in a cell or a cookie dropped into a pocket leaving the chowhall. There, at least, I was an individual with a name, not a stat with a number.

So it is true that here in the States the punishment is beyond physical confinement. It is more psychological. It is de-personalizing, dehumanizing. It is subtle and thorough and lasting — not a day goes by when I am not reminded of who I am, or by extension, of who I am not.

Which, paradoxically, is why I no longer think about escape. You could say that I've been broken, but I would describe it as "disappeared," and not for the worse. When I was in that Mexican prison I thought freedom was somewhere else, anywhere but there. More than anything, more than life, I wanted out. And when it happened, after the rush, what I discovered was not freedom but an overwhelming sense of emptiness and disappointment. There was a hollowness at my core that I never could have predicted, and I was desperate to fill it.

I took it personally. I worked harder, and worried more. I flew into rages. I left my wife and children, took risks I hadn't taken before. I thought it was a matter of more: more money, more possessions, more excitement. Freedom became a matter of distraction, anything that replaced the increasing certainty that there was no such thing as freedom, that there was, in fact, no way out of this greater prison I called my life.

The world felt heavier with each day, and I grew resentful in proportion. I assaulted total strangers, as if to take from them by force the innocence and contentment I could not conjure for myself. And I grew afraid. I thought I'd gone crazy, and in an effort to hide it I feigned normalcy with a precision that frightened me all the more. I became a phony even to myself.

Eventually, there seemed no cure but to kill myself or miraculously start over. And it was my arrest and this new experience of prison, this time in the States, that was the crucifixion, the beginning of the end of my beleaguered psyche. With the bad also went everything else, leaving me with nothing except what I could construct anew.

What came of this was the realization that freedom had nothing to do with the conditions and circumstances of my world. Mexico showed me the worst; there was an honesty in that revelation. It was crowded and filthy and dangerous, much like my thinking, and I yearned to be elsewhere. True, I was allowed to keep my identity, but it was an identity that was poisonous, and it took this long stretch of psychological deprivation in the U.S. to provide the ultimate wake-up call, the ontological slap in the face. The direction was clear: freedom was not out there, it was in here, inside me. What I had been yearning for all along was not a change in location but a change in outlook, and the solution would be found prior to my expectations, prior even to my beliefs. All I had to do was to see them for what they were: lies, mostly, recycled history, and most definitely obstructions to peace and contentment and compassion for others. I reasoned that, if I change, the world would reflect that change, and it has, even here.

So I am grateful for the time in that Mexican prison, and just as grateful for the long years in this state prison, strange as that may sound. And when a fellow convict asks if I've done time before and I tell him my little story about Mexico, I check closely for his reaction. It is not shock or revulsion I am looking for, it is desperation—how badly does he want it, how far will he go for his freedom, and in what direction?

For there is no formula for this turnaround. It happens to

some, and not to most. Usually, they shake their heads and maybe whistle through their teeth, and then like every other day, they go their way and I go mine.

Although I wish it were otherwise

LEAF

The guards told me about you when they led me to my cell. They called you Old Max because even their fathers who worked here before them couldn't remember when you arrived. They said you were as cold as time, hardened by these stone walls that held you all those years. They told me to stay away from you.

I remember the day I approached your cell, offering strong coffee in my deepest voice to impress you. I thought you were asleep with your eyes open—there on your metal bunk in that empty room, your thick, crusted arms at your sides like the rotting limbs of a fallen oak. You would not look at me. You did not move or speak . . . and yet I heard you; I heard you as clearly as if you had shouted. "Tell me about the trees," you said, "tell me about the trees"—over and over until I fled, searching for a way to stop the clamor of your gnarled voice in my head.

I did not understand, then. I thought you were mad. I avoided you, hiding throughout the long summer months in my tiny, boiling cell, sweating memories. There were young loves to recall. There were fast cars and quick deals, cool nights with hot money. There was the wild movie of my life, the fire of exploding youth—and you wanted to know about trees.

But the pictures of my past, like distant flashes of lightning in a passing storm, grew faint with the pale, crisp days of October. There was nothing then—nothing but the cold clank of iron doors,

17

the angry glare of naked bulbs on white cement. For the first time, I felt compelled to leave the building and visit the paved yard next to the cellhouse. For the first time, I wanted to see the sky.

I heard the wind that day, long before it arrived, thundering down the valley, scouring the fields nearby. Suddenly, pushing an army of leaves, it tumbled over the wall, then scurried wildly around the compound, spraying the woody scent of freedom carried from an alien and fenceless land beyond. And then it vanished as quickly as it had appeared, leaving only its secret.

Somehow I knew the message was for you, and when I looked at your window, open on its rusty hinges, I knew you were no longer there in the darkness of your cell. "Tell me . . . ," you said, your voice the last gasp of breeze slipping past the wall, ". . . tell me about the trees."

I ran, blinded by the stillness that followed; I ran as if the world had stopped and I had been shot forward by the momentum. I remember sprinting to the cellhouse door, then racing up the metal stairs to the third tier—each step a year of your past and a year of my future, each breath a scream of disbelief, refusing the certainty that the end for you was the beginning for me.

You were sprawled on the tier, face down, your outstretched arm thrust rigidly through the bars of my cell. "Gone," the guard said, pressing his hand to your neck. He looked at me, then reached through the bars and plucked the dead leaf from your lifeless fingers. It was an oak leaf, a mirage of clouded amber through my tears, the color of trapped time. He held it by the stem, turning it from side to side, then passed it to me. "Must have blown in with the wind," he said.

Thirty years have passed since that day. The leaf has long since crumbled and returned to dust. And yet the memory of your face, your voice, lives on in the clanging, grinding emptiness of this penitentiary. It is cold in this cell. Even though it is May, winter lurks in these dark rooms, refusing to leave. I have grown old lying on this hard bed, scratching the days on the wall, each successive mark a crude symbol of the present, a circular trail of endless moments penciled into concentric rings, a record of my age. They bring food to me, and years ago, they tried to coax me outside, but now they leave me alone. They think I am mad.

This morning a young convict, a newcomer to the prison, stopped and stared at me through the bars. I could see he wanted to talk; he wanted to tell me his tall tales of wild nights on the streets — or perhaps he wanted advice, words of wisdom from "Old Max."

But I could not listen to this boy's shallow dreams, and I had little to offer: I know less now about this prison than when I arrived. I stopped him before he started. I wanted to hear about cold streams on clear mornings, about endless fields of purple wildflowers, about grass. I wanted to know about the forests, especially the trees, great quilts of warm green trees.

I asked him, silently, to tell me about the trees.

PART TWO

HEADLESSNESS

"Why just ask the donkey in me
To speak to the donkey in you

When I have so many other beautiful animals
And brilliant colored birds inside that are longing to say
something wonderful and exciting to your heart?

Let's open all the locked doors upon our eyes
That keep us from knowing the intelligence
That begets love
And a more lively and satisfying conversation
With the Friend.

—Hafiz

PERFECTLY RIDICULOUSLY EASY

For years I had the strongest urge to discover something I couldn't define. It was as if I were being led into a maze by an unnamable source. It was, as the saying goes, like searching in a dark room for a black cat that wasn't there. Except I didn't know what I was searching for!

I was restless and confused, and although after college I tried to settle into the two-car suburban life, the urge persisted, and soon after, without trying, I found LSD (or it found me!). Of all the turning points in my life, in retrospect I have to say that this was the most significant. During that first trip, an opening appeared—of what I couldn't say—but an opening that thoroughly wiped the slate clean of everything I thought was real. There were more trips after that, but none had the power of the first, and then, strange as it seemed at the time, the opening I'd seen soon dwindled into questions of my sanity: Had I briefly gone mad? Was there something wrong with me? Had I given up on making something of my life?—for by then I had quit my brief foray into the corporate world and succumbed to the trap of drinking and carousing, no doubt to block the fear of having glimpsed something life-threatening, truly world-ending.

But the urge did not disappear. A decade and a half later, footloose and well into a life of criminal activity, and then finally with a major arrest and facing the prospect of a life in prison—or perhaps because of it—I found myself propelled headlong into the search, book after book on Taoism, Buddhism, Vedanta, the Sufis, Christian mystics and the Kabbala.

And eventually, with one simple look suggested by an English philosopher, I discovered why I previously didn't get it, and why others I encountered didn't get it. It was too simple, too easy, too close. All the searching and frustration and seemingly wasted energy, the thousand wells I had dug and the one deep one into Eastern religion, all a joke at which I could only laugh; there wasn't even an "I" that I could blame, nor even one to laugh with! And I had seen this, albeit momentarily, all those years ago in the days before the counterculture of the 1960s when I first dropped acid.

The story goes that the 13th Century trickster Mullah Nazrudin approached the border on a donkey one day. The border guard checked his papers and let him pass, but was suspicious of this strange man on his donkey. The next day when Nazrudin approached the border, the guard questioned him and searched his meager belongings, but found nothing, and soon let him pass. On the third and fourth days when Nazrudin approached, the guard meticulously examined him, but each time found nothing and had to let him go. By now, the guard was convinced that Nazrudin was smuggling something into the country, and every day thereafter when Nazrudin arrived at the border, he grew more and more frustrated when he found nothing. Finally, on the weekend when he was off duty and already a bit drunk, he ran into Nazrudin in a bar across the border. "Sir," he said. You are driving me crazy. Every day I search you coming across the border, and every day I find nothing. I don't know how you do it, but I know you are smuggling something. Please, I beg of you. I promise not to arrest you and I promise not to repeat this conversation to anyone, but tell me, what is it you are smuggling?"

"Donkeys," replied Nazrudin.

The obvious point of the tale is that awakening is so close we miss it, so obvious we fail to see it. I can't count the times in my life I have searched for my glasses only to find I was looking through them.

So it is with awakening. Where is the black cat in the dark room? It isn't there. It's here. It was never there because awakening is the recognition that what is looked for is what is looking! Which of course is always Here. "God" isn't out there somewhere, separate from you. Your eyes are His eyes, your awareness is His awareness, your sense of being, of presence, is His presence. In fact, Awareness/Presence is what God IS: pure, empty, silent awareness, capacious of all that appears, and all that appears does so in the only place it could appear, which is right Here where you are, where He is. There is no without. Never ever is anything "other," or "out there." As the 12th Century mystic Meister Eckhart put it, "God boils within Himself."

So boil. Get on with Who you really are, I say. What do you have to lose, except the lie of who you are not? What do you have to gain except everything? Come to Nothing, and find Everything.

WORDS GALORE

So many books, so much talk, so many words.

Read a novel, a magazine, a textbook, a newspaper, a how-to manual. Read for enjoyment, for distraction, to learn, to laugh, to titillate, to ponder.

Want to improve your mind, your attitude, your body? Read your choice of thousands of self-help books. How about a book on Mindfulness? Be in the moment, attend to the task at hand and relax your "monkey mind" and its bag of regrets about the past and worries for the future. You could have a happier, more fulfilling life, you could be "here and now."

The only problem is—and it happens to be a huge one—is that you still think there's a "you" that you can improve!

Ram Dass and several other awakened masters mean something entirely different when they point to Here and Now. What they are referring to has little or nothing to do with being in a "moment," since they are quite aware that, even if there were such a thing as a moment, you wouldn't be in it, it would be in You. To the awakened, Here/Now refers to that which is prior to space, prior to time, and prior to thought, totally inconceivable as a concept but exactly What You Really Are! Perhaps I could say that Here/Now refers to that no-moment of no space and no time, but what could that possibly mean? How to explain what can't be explained, yet is so obviously Who You Are? As Wei Wu Wei so often reminded us, it is like trying to conceptualize that which is conceptualizing!

Words simply won't do. And this is the genius of the aptly named "Headless Way." Words aren't necessary. In fact, they too often interfere. Occasionally they may skillfully point one toward the "gateless gate" of awakening, but mostly they do just the opposite and mire one all the more deeply in the confusion and confrontation of separation.

Douglas Harding's gift to the world is that he tells you to "look," not to believe him or anyone else, but to look for yourself, that you and only you are the final authority on what you find. And he also tells you where to look, which is 180 degrees the opposite of where you usually look. In other words, look "here" and not "out there." Attend to what you see when you look at what you're looking out of. And actually look, rather than think. For instance, look here where you think (!) you have a head and notice that you can't see it. Touch what you think is your head and notice that the sensations you feel don't add up to one, or for that matter, add up to anything! Take what you see here as real, not what you grew up innocently believing was here because others (your parents, siblings, relatives) told you what was here (from their point of view where they were, which was over there, they saw an object called a head and told you that you had one too. But now, present day, and on present evidence, take what you actually see as true, not what you see in the mirror over there or what others say they see from where they are over there or what cameras record from over there. After all, you're here, not over there!

My guess is that you see exactly what I see, which is nothing. The backbone of Buddhist wisdom traditions is "Emptiness," and whether you're a Buddhist or not you don't have to look far to find it. In fact, looking back, you see that you are it. How much more "empty" could you be? There is literally nothing here—no thing (object).

However, "emptiness" does not mean absolute absence, a total blank. It does not imply a nothing that is the opposite of a something. When I look here, I see boundless space, but a space that is aware, conscious, alive, and with a sense of presence, of I-AM-NESS. And it's not as if awareness/I-AM-NESS is inside the space; awareness/I-AM-NESS and this boundless space are the same! Seeing this, I've no doubt that this is what I am: Empty Awareness, birth-less and deathless and timeless. And seeing this, anyone can say the same, but it is crucial to SEE who you are first, then allow and affirm what is true for you. Seeing—the act of looking at looking—is pure unmediated experience. It has been called the only true experience because it is the experience of Itself, and it is always available, no matter the mood or circumstance.

First See that you are Aware Emptiness, right here where you once thought you had a head, and then, affirming that, notice that Aware Emptiness is also filled with the scene that you once thought was in front of you, "out there." It isn't, of course, it never was. It is within the Aware Empty Space here! Where is anything experienced, but here where you are. It is not experienced "over there," it is experienced here. When you see this, when you awaken to this, this too becomes unmediated true experience. This is Who You Really Are. You are both Empty Aware Space and the scene within it. This is the Buddhist formula, seen all at once: First there are mountains and rivers (everyday perception of objects as outside of who you think you are, a separate self-existing individual). Then there are no mountains and rivers (seeing you are Aware Emptiness). Then once again there are mountains and rivers (as inside you, and therefore as what you are). .

Seeing, this may happen immediately and all at once, or it may seem to happen in stages. In fact, there are no stages because Seeing is timeless, and is therefore always immediate. It only appears to happen in stages. You may notice that Seeing Who You Really Are is always the first time, no matter how many times you appear to do it and no matter how many ways you think you experience it. There are no levels to Seeing—you cannot do it better nor worse than anyone else, and therefore there are no beginners nor old experienced hands. The first time is always the same as the last time because there are no times.

And finally, if you still think you are located in a separate body and that this is all nonsense, look down at your body, take exactly what you see, and notice that it too happens to be inside this vast, empty and aware Space above your chest.

Welcome to Who You Really Are!

THE HOLY CIRCLE OF LIGHT

Snow today, and our Buddhist teacher didn't make it to our monthly meeting. He drives to this prison from the city, nearly two hours away, and when the weather is bad, we know we're on our own.

We fill the time with chit-chat to start, and then Chris, our inmate set-up man, a long-time member of our sangha who begins and ends our sessions when there is no teacher, raps the gong and we take the meditative position on our plastic chairs. We chant, then fall silent, eyes open, following our breath. The noise of the prison fades, the mind slows, and an opening appears, revealing this boundless emptiness where I once thought I had a head. Thoughts quietly arise and pass away in this awake space.

And then abruptly—it can't have been more than ten minutes—Chris raps the gong again, and we lean back in our chairs, stretch our arms and legs, still silent.

He poses the question: "How do each of you get through your day?"

The answers come slowly—grudgingly, it seems—like something you'd hear at a prison AA meeting where no one does the steps: Jack works all day, Brian reads a lot, Eddie watches TV and exercises, Al works, then plays cards until lockdown at 9:30 P.M. Of the eight of us, not one mentions meditation, although two claim they study Buddhist dharma. When it's my turn, I suddenly realize I am not mentally prepared, so I blurt out, "I don't get through the day, the day gets through Me."

No one looks my way, as though I'm not there. I want to explain that, actually, I'm not, but something tells me it's not the time, although maybe the place. It occurs to me, however, that deep beneath the façade they erect, they already know that who they pretend to be isn't Who They Really Are, and Who They Really Are isn't anywhere. For it is only to others that we appear as an object, and as babies when we innocently accepted what others said they saw from where they were rather than what we saw from where we were, we unwittingly made objects of our One Self and became instead "ourselves," resulting in the current belief that we are each a tiny inconsequential speck separate from and up against a vast and mostly hostile universe—a belief that may well have been necessary in the development of an ego (for after all, with no ego there would be no story, no "life," no objective world), but a primal mistake nonetheless.

And how do I know I am not that now? How do I know I am not an inconsequential speck located somewhere inside an unfathomably vast universe? I See I am not. Looking back at what is looking—that is, reversing my attention 180 degrees and taking exactly what I see and not what I think or have been told by others—I see only empty and boundless space, a space that is not only aware but aware it is aware, a space that is not only empty but is filled with the scene, and filled in such a way that the "void" of this emptiness and the "form" of the scene are the same—I can find no difference between the empty awareness and the scene within it. I am awake to this. I am present as this. I am nothing, a nothing that is completely still as no-thing (for what could there be to move?), and a nothing that is at the same time 100 percent filled with the ever-changing and on-the-move scene that includes all perceptions and sensations and the thoughts attached to them. Looking within, how could this be doubted? What else could I be? I see I am not an object among an infinite number of objects, but that all so-called "objects" appear inside this Empty Awareness that I am, appear *in* and therefore *as* what I am. Objects are not objects, they are what I am—Subject! Objects are not separate from Me or from each other, they are my only reality as "I," the only thing I can be said to be!

The conversation about "getting through the day" dwindles to a stop, and Chris suggests a bit of yoga instruction from Tony. We move the chairs and stand in a large circle. Tony begins with easy poses he calls "old man's yoga," and I am grateful for this warmup to the more difficult poses which I cannot do. Later during the hard part when Eddie falls over on his back and assumes the pose of roadkill, limbs frozen in rigor mortis, we all laugh in un-yoga-like sprawls, then finally stand and retrieve the chairs and sit back down.

Chris rings the gong, and we settle into more meditation. Another ten minutes pass, and he calls for *Tonglen*, a practice whereby, breathing in, we take in the suffering of others, and breathing out, we breathe out peace and happiness to them. We do this for loved ones and for enemies, then do the same for those we don't know in an ever widening circle of imagination, eventually offering compassion with each out-breath to all beings everywhere. We learn empathy, this way, a concept in short supply in prison, and, according to what we see on TV news, in short supply just about everywhere else, as well.

When we finish, I ask if everyone would like to try something different, and they all nod. I tell them to form a circle and place their arms around each other's backs. Eddie and Al crack a few "I'm secretly embarrassed but please don't tell anyone" jokes, and then we fall silent. To begin, I ask that we all continuously intone the deep sound of "om," breathing in quickly and intoning out, over and over until the impetus to do so fades. We do this for five minutes, and finally the sound and the resonance gently drift into silence, and we stand in the quietude of newness.

"Look down," I say. "See where we all have individual bodies: feet, legs, torsos. Keep looking down, and at the same time notice what's above our bodies, above yours and everyone else's. Take a look, and take exactly what you see, not what you think you should see.

"I'll tell you what I see. I see Space, nothing, no-thing at all. I see no heads, no head here nor anywhere above any of the bodies in this circle. Our separate appearances down there may be connected in this circle, but here where we thought we each had a head, aren't we all One Space, One Emptiness, totally the same because there is nothing, not one thing, to be different? Thoughts may arise, but what is it they arise in? Perceptions may be on view, but where are they seen? Where do you actually experience anything? Is it not in this Space that all perceptions and sensations and mentations arise and pass? Aren't you, as Aware Empty Space, the context, the container of all things, all thoughts, all feelings—and in such a way that the Aware Space and what fills it are wedded as One? Hasn't it always been this way?"

At first, no one says a word, and then Eddie lets out a nervous chuckle which signals the break-up of the circle, and everyone finds their chair. I know that we all saw the emptiness above our bodies, but only Eddie looks stunned by it. He stares at me, and I can tell he is looking not only at me but what he is looking out of, what we are all looking out of all the time: not two eyes enclosed in a head but a vast, boundless openness of absolutely No-thing, wide awake.

Later as we are leaving he says to me, "What *is* that?" which is the same question I've asked myself countless times and the same question I've heard from others who suddenly see their own Light, even if they still think it's their own.

"I don't know," I say. "There are many names for it—Buddha, God, Self, Beloved, Tao, Basic Space of Awareness—but these say nothing. They are labels, mere representations for what you yourself have actually seen, and seeing is wordlessly experiencing, not to mention believing."

"Well, what do *you* call it?"

"It depends on who is listening. What I see when I look at what I am looking out of is Nothing—no eyes, no face, no head— simply Nothing, or better yet, No-thing, a No-thing that is at the same time filled with the scene, so that I can say that I see Nothing/Everything, right here where I am and no one else is.

This is so obvious, and so overlooked—yet it is so obviously what I am. And it's aware. That's the kicker, isn't it? It's aware—and what is that? How did that happen? It's a mystery, the mystery of all mysteries, and it's what I am, my true Self. I see that I am not the separate body/mind/individual I thought I was. Frankly, it blows my mind—that is, when contraction happens and I think I am my mind."

"How do you stop the contraction?"

"That's a strange question because it assumes there's a 'you' who can do so. Not only that, but it assumes there's a way or a method that can accomplish it. Looking back at what is looking, what is seen? I see nothing, filled with the scene, and along with it a sense of presence, of I-am-ness. All I can say is that what I see is a boundless openness of absolutely No-thing in which anything and everything appears. So I'll say it's the One—or whatever you want to call it—that calls the shots. A "you" has nothing to do with it. 'Hows' and 'Whys' have no place in this vision of Who You Really Are by Who You Really Are."

Eddie thanks me, and we part, he to his cellhouse and I to mine in a different part of the prison. I wish that weren't the case because I immediately feel a kinship with him, but it is what is, and I know that what is is perfect (or it wouldn't be what is!).

On the way, I run into Michael who is adorned with multicolored tattoos head to toe, one of the few prisoners I've seen whose body more resembles a moving canvas of artistic expression rather than the usual displays of power and death. He is not a Buddhist, but he came to our group meeting one day to tell me that he read my book and tried the headless experiments and "got it" right away, and since then, it has changed his outlook. I am always pleased to see him. He is as lit up and enthusiastic as any man I have met. It's good to know that the Beatific Vision of Douglas Harding is the same vision of so many others now, the vision of Who We All Really Are as One.

NO-MINDFULNESS

You practice mindfulness. You have read the books and dabbled in the scriptures; you joined a Buddhist *Vipassana* group and practice insight meditation. Now you go around trying to be "aware."

There is something to be said for this mindfulness, of course. How much easier it should be to live in the present, with less guilt from the past and less worry for the future. You can, as they say, be present in the Now, and hence live more fully, moment by moment. After all, if you are not mindful, you are mindless—thus, how can you "wear out the shoe of samsara?"

Ah, but it isn't easy, you discover. This living in the present seems unnatural at first. How can one possibly be aware all the time? But with practice, lots and lots of meditation, sitting and otherwise, you develop the ability to hold your awareness for longer and longer periods, sometimes for part of a day. "This is Buddhism," you think. "This is the way." Eventually you'll be fully "awake"—for what else could "awake" mean but to be mindful all the time. And already you have become more peaceful, you function better, you appreciate more; you have even learned to take a step back, to watch yourself, to let things happen and thus douse the fires of your prideful will, to allow compassion in—certainly your life has become more meaningful. But is this all there is? Is this the Buddhist ideal? Is one, in fact, "awake" because one is one hundred percent in the present?

The answer arrives one day when you happen to read a passage in a book on Buddhist metaphysics about "time"—what it is, or rather, what it isn't—and something inside you snaps. The past and future, you are told, are in your head, one as memory, and the other as imagination. But the present, because of the complicated biochemical processing of sense perceptions, which of course takes time, is already in the past by the time you experience it! You are—you realize all too clearly!—living in the past, albeit a recent one, which happens to be in your head! Or perhaps you are living in the future, which you can never know until it has become the past. Where, in any case, is this precious "present" you have for so long been practicing to be present in?

And so you wonder: If all that you see and hear and touch is in your head, then just what is it you are "aware" of? Where, or when, does "mindfulness" come in? What difference is there, in the Large View, between being mindful and being mindless? So what if you are daydreaming—is that any more or less true to your real nature than being mindful? After all, they are both in your head!

Now suddenly years of practice—your great investment in what you thought was the present—are called into question. You find yourself feeling hollow, fearful, and even angry. This everyday world, what you have been paying close attention to, is somehow not there as you thought it was. And then it dawns on you that if the world is not there as you thought, perhaps you are not there as you thought! How strange—here you are, a fictitious "you" being mindful of a fictitious world in a fictitious present, and all of it a product of "your" imagination! Now, not only does the question arise: What is there to be mindful of? But alas, who is there to be mindful of it?

What to do? The inquiry sits like a rock at the bottom of your teacup. If, as you have heard and as you now wish were not so forcefully clear, there is no "you," and likewise no "other-than-you," what in the lost world is all this fuss about mindfulness?

The solution strikes you as exceedingly humorous—the very idea that there could be something to fuss about, the idea that there could be anyone to do something about anything! In fact, there is no answer because the question is not really a question.

And with that realization comes a shift of consciousness, a somersault, the miraculous metanoia you have read about. Now mindfulness is suddenly "no-mindfulness" — mindfulness in its true sense — not a "you" in the "present" but simply an all-embracing Presence.

It is a Presence that you (but not as a "you") are creating, moment by precious moment. What you once called "time" you now see for what it is — a concept — so the past, the future, and even the biochemical process itself, are revealed as conceptual interpretations of what is basically a "timeless Presence (presented serially), Here and Now intemporally. Creating the world constitutes the Here and Now — the process itself is the so-called "present."

Aware of this, you are also aware of Subjectivity, for to "create the world" and to "perceive the world" must necessarily be the same; they cannot be separate. There is, you realize, no such thing as subject seeing objects, because seer and seen are one and the same. This is the realization, the (sort of) awareness that is "mindfulness," the no-mindfulness (for there is no one to be mindful of no-separate thing) that is true mindfulness.

Mindfulness, after all, is Mindfulness being mindful of Mindfulness. Need you say more?

LETTER TO A FRIEND

Awhile back I came across an article in Discover magazine entitled "Astronomy at the Speed of Light" (by Bob Berman, December, 2005, p.24) that caught my attention, in particular this one sentence:

"A photon does not pass through time at all: Travelling at the speed of light, it experiences being everywhere in the universe all at once."

And not long after, I read much the same in The Little Book of Life and Death, in which the late English philosopher Douglas Harding quotes John Gribbon from Gribbon's book In Search of Schrodinger's Cat:

"At the speed of light time stands still; to a photon the Big Bang and the present are the same time. Therefore the universe is connected by a web of electro-magnetic radiation which 'sees' everything at once."

During the last thirty years or so there have been several popular books published for the lay public on the subject of the new physics and cosmology. But of those that I've read, not one proffered the suggestion that light is the Observer, Consciousness, Who We Really Are—this, despite numerous pronouncements on how we are required to radically rethink our views of reality, or despite millennia of references to Light by the great spiritual traditions. But how else can one interpret the conclusions of relativity and quantum mechanics? For the facts point to the observer. Einstein's mass/energy equation tells us that our universe and our world of everyday objects—this paper and this ink, for instance—are, in fact, energy. And energy, as quantum mechanics points out, whether chosen to be "seen" as a wave or a particle, is no more than a measure of its position when observed; beyond this, it cannot be said to exist. Objects "collapse" into apparent "reality" only when observed.

Moreover, relativity theory demonstrates that space and time and mass are relative to the motion of the observer, and in this way depend upon the observer. The speed of light, however, is constant (as is Einstein's space/time invariant, a mathematical combination of space and time demonstrating that changes in space relate to changes in time), regardless of whether the observer is moving toward an object or away from it. But does this not call into question the premise of "observer" and "observed" (not to mention the assumption of multiple universes), or at least provide a clue to the possibility that the distinction may be illusory? Would it not be simpler to explain the paradoxes of relativity theory if there were only one Observer with multiple space/time "views?" Or no observer, apart from that which is observed? Only observing? *

For what is light but what One is, and what is the space/time invariant but a measure of how One appears as the universe? What I Am is spacelessly and timelessly the center of the universe because all of space/time is what I manifest as. Space and time have no reality other than this. What the new physics therefore suggests is that only the observer "exists," and given this, it becomes clear as to where space and time and all of matter originate. There are no fixed and intrinsically existing properties called "space" and "time." There are only events of observation, the Observer observing Himself, and in the process, weaving His measurements into an appearance of reality. Quantum imaginers, What We Are "collapses" repetitively, instant by instant from the stillness of probability into our manifestation as time, assigning these instants, these "quanta," to what we call "light"—that mystery we cannot otherwise define because it is what we are. Is this not perhaps the way, science's way, to define "enlightenment?"

ON DYING

Melvin, my octogenarian friend with his share of dementia, has now reached the stage where the distinction between TV reality and so-called "real" reality has significantly blurred. Recently a friend caught Melvin waving to a game show model who had waved goodbye to the audience at the end of the show. And I too have seen him, wide-eyed and on the edge of his bunk, mouthing inaudible words to a cross-eyed bird in a Saturday morning cartoon. I love this old guy, and I hope that when I'm his age I'll at least enjoy life as much as he seems to, never complaining, never blaming or belittling others, never rejecting whatever shows up. Only once have I ever heard him utter a negative word, and that was in regard to an apparent relationship he'd had with the Prince of Darkness. "Before I came to prison," he told me, "oh, the devil was in me!"

These days more than ever I think about dying. Or living longer. Quickly followed, thank goodness, by how absurd those notions are, for what is there but this body, this brief apparition, that could do either? Here, right where I am, I see nothing but awareness. No "thing" at all, and it is only things — objects appearing in awareness — that can live or die, each and all of them arising and passing expressions of this aware no-thing that I am. And yet, despite the fact that awareness both witnesses and is what it witnesses (and knows that that is what it is!), it also seems to forget, and in the forgetting continues to play this marvelous game of oneness pretending to be twoness. Could there be an adventure more wildly improbable yet so completely satisfying? So endlessly new, yet always the same?

A neighbor here is slowly killing himself. He's a devout Christian, he claims he's not depressed, and he's convinced that only by dying will he find himself in a better place. Of course, to him, suicide is an unforgivable sin, but he's figured out a way around that by trying to eat himself into a heart attack or cancer. He's morbidly obese. He gobbles almost nothing but cake and cookies and whatever packaged junk food he can afford from our weekly canteen, conveniently forgetting that gluttony is also a sin, and could, in his worldview, send him to the place he least wants to go.

Which reminds me of a joke. Hugh Hefner and Madonna die and meet Saint Peter at heaven's gate. Saint Peter tells Hugh Hefner that, because he corrupted so many young men's minds with pictures of nude women in his magazines, in order for him to get into heaven he will have to walk through a tunnel, and if he has one impure thought, a trap door will open and he'll fall through to hell. So Hugh Hefner walks into the tunnel, with Saint Peter 10 feet behind. Halfway through, Saint Peter yells out, "Naked breasts!" —and immediately a trap door opens and Hugh Hefner falls through to hell.

Back at the gate, Saint Peter tells Madonna that she too must walk through the tunnel, and because she corrupted so many young men's minds with her sensuous moves, if she has one impure thought, a trap door will open and she'll fall through into hell. So Madonna starts into the tunnel with Saint Peter 10 feet behind. Halfway into the tunnel a trap door suddenly opens, and Saint Peter falls through.

Sadly, from my neighbor's point of view of a separate "self" confronting a separate world, this is no joke. To him and to so many others, life is a never-ending struggle of failing to live up to one's distorted beliefs and then having to suffer the consequences of a presumed afterlife based on either how great or how little one failed (or, as in Buddhism, suffering an endless succession of presumed reincarnations).

Added to that is the fact that, when you finally do "see the light" (!), you find out that you never left it, that it was this assumed "you" that all along was the joke, a "you" that was never in the central spot to begin with, a "you" who never had the power to get it wrong, a "you" that could never do anything at all, apart from the All of No-thing/Everything.

And how much easier this so-called "living" should be when the false ideas of life and death are seen through, or, as Wei Wu Wei once said, when you finally board the train and leave your baggage behind. And so it is. So it all is when this timeless and boundless and empty Aware Capacity for everything arising and passing is seen, actually seen, and therefore indisputably known to be the true Self.

Two weeks ago Melvin collapsed on the sidewalk in front of the medical clinic, and by the time they got him inside, he was flatlined. Somehow they revived him and got him to a hospital where he underwent bypass surgery, and now he's back, looking pale and more stooped than ever as he trudges to the chowhall, towing an oxygen tank on wheels. Today he told me that everyone keeps asking how he's doing (to which he always answers what he really believes, which is "Fine!"), so I related to him what I'm fond of saying when someone asks me that question: that I'm like the guy who fell off the roof of a ten story building and was heard to say as he passed each floor, "So far, so good!" — to which Melvin chuckled, so I added, "I'm at the second floor, Melvin."

"Yeah," Melvin said. He had a funny look on his face, as if he were confused about something, like maybe he was wondering whether or not he was confused. Then he slowly looked down, moistened his lips, and half-whispered something that truly amazed me.

"I think I already hit the bottom floor," he said. "But it wasn't there."

WILL THE REAL J.C. PLEASE STAND UP!

Sri Swami Baba Muktananda said, "The highest purpose we have in this life is to recognize our own Awareness of Being as the universal Self which has become everyone. The primary process in life is not of becoming but recognizing what already is."

I could say that Baba Muktananda is right. And I could say that Baba Muktananda is wrong.

But who am I to comment on the perfectly right or wrong words of Baba Muktananda? I'm nobody. In fact, I'm NOBODY. The very same NOBODY/NO-THING that has no thoughts, no beliefs, and certainly no such thing as "purpose" for anybody or anything. And yet, all bodies, things, and purpose arise TO, WITHIN, and AS what I am. What else is there to recognize? And who is there apart from It to recognize It? What else could there be?

So who am I?

Is it not just THIS—Pure Awareness of Being, appearing as anything?—and can we leave it at that?

IMPROMPTU AWAKENING

This is the realization: You are dreaming, and the entire universe is your dream. Everyone else is a character in your dream. You have made them up. You have conjured every last person and thing in the cosmos because, after all, you are dreaming it. You are alone. You have always been alone and always will be alone, because there cannot be anyone else.

There is more to the realization: The world is a hoax, a sham, a cruel hallucination. The monumental superstructures of religion, science, culture—it is all a trick of the mind. Everything you held dear—your family, your home, your job, your friends, your town, your nation, the earth, "life"—is all a show, an incredibly intricate and complicated drama you have somehow created. It is the Great Joke. You could almost laugh, if it weren't blowing your mind.

Yes, you are afraid. You want desperately to be somebody—anybody—but now you know better. Now you can't go back. You can't go back because you realize there is not anywhere or anywhen to go back to. There is only Here and Now and This, and you don't know how to deal with all Three or all One or all None because they aren't a place, a time or a thing. You are afraid not because of what you have lost but because of what you are losing moment by moment. You are even afraid of being stuck in your fear—thoughts swirling madly like a horrifying carnival ride you can't get off. There is, you think, no way out.

But out to where? . . .

To Here! You know the answer, of course, and you also know that all you have to do is let go —but it seems so final, so "forever." Your head feels a little strange; you seem to be viewing the world from a little farther behind your eyes than usual, and you have the odd but certain conviction that everything you see is only you — which you really don't know what to do about. It dawns on you that, in fact, there is nothing you can do about it, never could and never will, because you, you realize, have nothing to do with it, for you too are a character in your dream. Then who is dreaming?

You are! My God, you are alone, and the greatest joke of all is that you have dreamed up a "you," someone who thought to be in charge, responsible for your every move and a few moves of "others" as well. But there is no "you," there are no "others," there is only the dreaming (no dreamer and nothing dreamed), so what to do?

Now you do laugh, and while you are laughing you watch yourself laugh —it is all so hilarious, this "doing." What could you or anyone else possibly do? And this "seeing" —what possibly could one see that is not the seer?

A wave of gratitude washes over you. The fear is gone, and even if it were to return you feel you would be grateful for it too. Now there really are things to do, an unlimited supply of "doing,' all without a "you," all presenting themselves with a smile. It is as before but so completely different. Alone? You? The idea is as absurd as there being a "you" to be alone! How could you have been so blind, so ignorant? You could dance, you feel so light. Dance with "reality," the only reality there is, the reality you have created. Dance with yourself! Oh endless laughter and waves and waves of —what? Bliss? Joy? —gushing from within. So this is the realization! This is it? This is all it is? No mystery, no hidden meanings, no secret of secrets, just the profound apprehension that the seer is the seen, and the seen is the seer!

So it is, you think. And with that, you realize that now it is just a thought —somehow, the "experience" has passed, as all experiences do, and you are left with a memory, an abstraction, a

DON'T MIND ME!

I have no mind, not here. It's "out there" frolicking in the world, as the world. Here, I see only clear space with no qualities, simply no-thing and no "mind" (whatever a "mind" could be). The scene appears, thoughts pass through, but always the thoughts are attached to the scene, part and parcel of the things that comprise the scene; never are they "mine," contained in an imaginary head here above my torso where, if I tell the truth—the truth being the way I truly experience it right now in this moment—I see no head, no such place for thoughts to hang out and cause problems. Thoughts are attached to and belong to the things of this world, are the things of this world. This includes all thoughts—mental images, memories, dreams, beliefs—anything that can be said or named. "I" is one such thought, attached to this flesh body that others call "J.C." When I say "my mind" (and believe it), a fundamental mistake is made, that of being a separate and self-existing individual with certain thoughts that occur here and only here in this head and nowhere else at this particular time and place. In this scenario, the statement "my mind" refers to a storage house of thoughts, beliefs, memories, expectations, imaginations, etc., that lurk inside this head waiting to be called upon or to call upon "me," to control or be controlled by "me," to upset the cart or set it aright.

But how easy and relaxing it is to let thoughts simply be thoughts, to know they aren't "mine" but instead are attached to things, to all the objects and images arising and passing, appearing moment by moment, floating by.

Here, I am free of them, I can watch them, allow them, enjoy them. Here, I need not follow them, attach to them, own them. Here, I can be surprised or amazed or grateful beyond measure for them (for without thoughts, there would be no "world"). Here, I can love them, see them as perfect and perfectly faultless. Here, they are What I Am, appearing as That. They are the drama of my life, all the ups and downs and rights and lefts rolled into one, a performance I never would have (nor could have) missed.

I see an object called a "tree." As a child I learned from others that it is named a tree, so now it is a tree. The thought "tree" and all the secondary qualities related to that thought are attached to the object, experienced here and now as a "tree." It is not "my" thought, apart from the object. I am not separately responsible for the thought, I am not right or wrong because I personally thought it. My head is not packed with thoughts that should or should not be there. And why? I have no room for such nonsense because I have no head! In its place I find the world, a world of things, with thoughts and feelings attached to them, all arising and passing by, the continuous movement of Stillness Itself, Pure Subjectivity, Awake Emptiness functioning as things-passing-by.

To get used to this, to make it permanent, takes practice, and I find that looking in at the empty aware space that I am while simultaneously looking out at the scene, or what Douglas Harding called "two-way looking," is the most effective way. It is immediate and unmediated. It is mindfulness in action, and while at first it may seem unnatural, ultimately one relaxes into the peace and extraordinary sense of freedom of the moment, and to the immediacy of what is meant by "Here," the only place one has ever been, which, ultimately, is no place at all.

With the index finger of one hand, point back at where you see no face, no head, no-thing above your chest, and with the index finger of the other hand, point out at whatever scene presents itself in your view. Whether you are indoors or outdoors makes no difference. Notice that the thoughts attach to the objects of the scene, and that they and the objects are presented together as one and the same, right here, right now. There is no distance between the objects in the scene and the thoughts or feelings about the objects. There is no distance (and no difference) between the objects in the scene and the aware space in which they appear. The aware space, the scene, and the thoughts and feelings are One, and nowhere in that equation is there a "you" to own any or all! It just is, and you can no longer take responsibility for the thoughts and feelings that are part and parcel of that scene because when you "see" that what you are looking at and what you are looking out of are the same, you realize that even "you" are a thought, an idea, a belief attached to a body-thing. The "mind" you thought you had is simply a collection of thoughts attached to an image you learned as a child, the image of a "you," itself a thought. That image was learned from others—parents, siblings, teachers, friends—according to what they saw from where they were, at a distance from you. It is not what you saw at your center, from where you were, and not what you see at your center today. It was an innocent mis-take of your identity, one you couldn't help but make as a child, especially at such a young age and especially when the "other" happened to be your mother or father. It was also a necessary mistake for socialization, and certainly required in order to survive as a member of the human community, but now it is time to come home to Who you really are, home to exactly what you see—or don't see—at the core of your being. Look back, turn your attention 180 degrees from where you habitually look, turn from exclusively viewing the scene "out there" to inclusively viewing the aware space filled with the world, all right here, where you are.

Where is your mind? Do you have a mind? Can you see it? Or when you look, do you find nothing of the sort, or of any sort? Telling the truth based on your senses and not your thoughts, in place of a so called "mind," might you not find simply awake emptiness filled with objects passing through, objects that constitute what we are calling the "scene," along with the thoughts and feelings that are attached to those objects?

Or perhaps for you it is as it was for me, the passing scene being not always so passing. That all-too familiar object called "my body" kept presenting itself, along with the firmly attached thought that this indeed was "me," chock full with all manner of secondary thoughts and feelings such as regrets, guilt, fear, worry, not to mention an excess of "shoulds" and "shouldn'ts" that imprisoned me for most of my life.

Until finally I looked, and when I looked, I stopped believing the lies, not all at once but eventually once and for all. Two-way looking is the answer, I say, and going by what you see, not what you think, and certainly not what "everyone else" says—this is end of confrontation and separation, and the beginning of wisdom.

GRACE

The tough guys here used to call themselves "convicts" and the rest of us "inmates." Some still do, and no doubt as a way to flex in front of the mirror of their insecurities. But a decade ago the staff throughout the state began officially calling us "offenders," to most of us an offensive name if ever there was one. And now, rather than "cons" or "ex-cons," we are forever "offenders" or "ex-offenders," terms that, because of their novelty if nothing else, alienate us even further from the mainstream of the public psyche. I once wrote a piece for a prison magazine defining "offender" as a wheel cover for an Irish car (pronounced O'fender), or alternatively as an "off-ender," one who has been pushed off the cliff of life. Needless to say, it was censored by the staff before the magazine went to print.

I suppose the majority of us take for granted the ad-speak and gov-speak we hear daily, but for prisoners it's hard to take seriously the word "Corrections." We are housed in a "Correctional Facility" by the "Department of Corrections," and few of us can figure out what it is that is corrected and how the State could take credit for it. "Penitentiary" might be a better word, but not, of course, as the Quakers intended it back in the days before our nation became a nation, when a penitentiary was a place to do penance. "What's wrong," we prisoners ask, "with the word 'prison'?" Who but the spin doctors would fault the honesty of calling it what it is, and wouldn't a fearful and clamoring public endorse the prospect of sending criminals to "prisons" or even "dungeons" for their crimes? Where are the Howard Cosells when we need them?

There are programs here that we offenders can take, such as Mental Health and GED and Drug & Alcohol, and one or two Therapy Communities we might qualify for, as well. With the right attitude a man can learn something, and his behavior may or may not change. But years ago a priest friend told me that any meaningful change in one's life could only arrive through the intervention of God. I had doubts then, but these days I know he was right.

When I first arrived here I was afraid, confused, lonely, anxious and ashamed. I think everyone enters prison this way, although most suppress it or cover it with bravado. Why else would a man or woman join a gang?

However, considering my former life of crime, the surprise to me was that these feelings prompted me to go straight. It's true that many men who come to prison seek God, in one form and in one religion or another, and I was no different, except that I bypassed the major religions and went straight for the heart of them all, the message that emerged in India and China long before the birth of Christ and was more recently popularized as the "Perennial Philosophy" by the English philosopher Aldous Huxley (in a book by that title), a philosophy which today is more often referred to as "Non-duality." I guess I can say that in the process (and many years into my sentence) I became a Buddhist for convenience, mainly because it seemed to offer a story closest to the truth, a description of the empty awareness that lies buried deep within the layers of religious custom. But I wanted more than ceremony, more even than the recommended practice. Meditation calmed my "monkey mind," relaxed my body and relieved stress, and later even brought me to the entrance of the "gateless gate."

But still I wanted to know, I wanted to pass through, I yearned for conclusive answers to the questions Who am I?, What is life?, What is this universe?

The answer came when I read one short article and did one simple (and I mean simple!) "experiment," as Douglas Harding called it. I pointed at where I thought I had a face, then told the truth. And the truth at that moment was that I saw no face, no anything. For all of my life, at least all of it that I remembered, I believed I had a face, but in actuality, when I put the belief aside that I had learned as a child from others and actually looked for myself, looked right here where I was, and looked using only the awareness and attention of the present moment, I saw nothing, simply a space so vast and so empty it contained everything, the entire scene before me. And I saw Awareness here. Not an awareness, an object, one that an "I" could claim (for what is an "I" but a thought, and all thoughts are objects) but only Awareness, and amazingly, Awareness aware of Itself, and simultaneously aware of Itself as Being or Presence, the indisputable answer to the question, Who am I? And at that instant, I knew why the gate had no gate, never did, never will.

So when I say that God has had a hand in what I think and feel and act, it is always more than that. I am what He thinks and feels, and from this wide-open Center these hands and feet do His bidding, performing moment by moment this radical transformation that dissolves my identity and merges it with His.

And while others may see me as an offender in a correctional facility, I don't see that here and now where God and I share this Being, this solitary and all-inclusive Presence. Everything changed when I saw the world inside Me, including this correctional facility, these thoughts and feelings and this upside-down body dressed in State clothes (should you see exactly what you see, not what you are conditioned to see, you may find that you too are upside-down!). And to this day, how marvelously freeing it is to see This and know that I am Nothing-at-All, that I am always Here where only God dwells, God who is both capacity for and the source of everything, even this prison—especially this prison.

TO HAVE AND TO HOLD

"You can't have everything. Where would you put it?"
—comedian Steven Wright

It's a funny joke told in his deadpan manner, but he's right, isn't he?

Oh but you can have everything!

Yeah, sure. So where would I put it?

Right where you are! Right in the Awake Void that accepts all and rejects nothing, where everything arises and passes as yours and no one else's, where you are the Sole Owner of every appearance that you alone simultaneously create and experience within.

But even if you could have everything, you wouldn't have time for it all, so what would be the point?

Oh but you would have time. And you do!

Like when?

Right now. And now, and now, and now. And since now is the only time there ever is, how could you not have time for it? Even if you think you don't have time, you're having time for the thought that you don't have time, and that thought happens to be "everything" at that moment. You see? The fact is, you cannot not have time for everything. There's no way out of this. This is not optional. What it ultimately comes down to is the fact that You as Who You Really Are, which is Empty Aware Capacity, are like an unblemished mirror that at every now-moment accepts everything and rejects nothing and has no choice but to do just that. And the "everything" that appears is not only the objects of the scene but the thoughts and feelings attached to those objects. This is Who You Are, and this is what you do. Or rather, appear to do.

What do you mean, "Appear to do?"

Because Who You Are doesn't really do anything. It's simply a case of being. There is no doing. In this instance, doing implies a spurious "you" to do it, and there is no such "you." That too is a thought attached to the appearance of the flesh body, a thought propped up by the assumption of having an individual "mind," which is another thought. The combination, often called "body-mind," is merely a tangled knot of thoughts which we could call a "me-belief." It is unsupported by the facts. There is no such thing. One look in the right direction will prove it.

So the "you" is part of the scene, part of the world, what you're referring to as "everything."

Exactly!

Then who am I?

If you mean who you think you are, you aren't!

Well, I'm not nothing. I've got to be something!

Yes and no. That "something" is not a "thing." I use the term Awareness, or Empty Awareness, because when I look back at what I am looking out of, or in other words, when I am aware of Awareness, I see nothing objective, no thing at all, simply an emptiness, or void, that has the quality—if you can call it a quality—of being aware, awake, alive, present. So it's not an absolute nothing, which is the opposite of something. It's a nothing the likes of which can't be described, except to say it is both void and aware, and moreover, aware it's aware.

Self-aware?

Yes, as long as you capitalize the "S." As long as you don't refer to it as an individual "self" separate from all other selves, which is a thought, a mistaken identity.

You said it can't be described, and yet you've described it as both void and aware.

Which maybe I shouldn't have. I can't describe it because it's not an object, and only objects can be described. I can't describe something that's not there and yet mysteriously is, but not as a "something." It can't be described because, you see, it's what is describing!

It's subject, not object.

Yes, but not "subject" as the opposite of "object." This can be confusing at first, which is why it is better to actually look and not use words, and when we look at where we thought we had a face and see no face—when we actually place our attention there—we may see a void that is more than just a void, it is an awake void, if you will. In other words, we see nothing there, but also see that it is aware, conscious, alive, present. So it is not simply nothing, it is a very special nothing right at the core of our being. Many have called this nothing by various names such as Pure Awareness, the Buddha-mind, God, Brahman, the Great Spirit, etc., but for this explanation let's use "No-thing," thereby distinguishing it from our usual concept of nothing as the opposite of something. Next, having established that, we look out upon the scene where we usually look. We can now make the distinction of "No-thing" being "here," and the scene, or "Everything," being "out there," and as I said, this is only for the purpose of bringing our attention away from where it is usually focused, which has been on the world "out there."

At that's it?

Not quite. The final step is Subject seeing only Subject, both Void and Form as one, No-thing and Everything as identical, which is Pure Subjectivity, the eternal Now.

When I look back at where I don't see my face, I can see that the no-thing here is aware, but I can't see that chair over there as the same as this aware void. What are you saying, that the chair is here?

Yes, but here as what you are! Combining aware No-thing here and the available scene there, we see that the scene is inside aware No-thing here. We are Space, or Capacity, for the scene, such that we cannot separate the one from the other. The scene appears within this No-thing that we are. Look. Forget what you've been told about where that chair is. Look at both Empty Awareness and the chair appearing within it. Try to separate the two and you can't. This is because they are not two! This is true of any object, any scene, the world, everything. No-thing and Everything appear together, always here, always now.

I kind of see that, but my mind is kicking up a storm. It just seems so impossible!

Yes, the mind can't accept the obvious because it ultimately means that the mind is no longer in charge. Really, it's better not to try to figure this out. Eventually it is seen. Actually, it doesn't matter whether it is seen or not because, no matter what, this is the way you are — there is no separation ever, never was, never will be. There is simply Pure Subjectivity. When we are very young children, a fundamental but perhaps necessary lie is passed down to us by our parents, siblings, and society, and that lie is the "original sin," the separation of "me" as an individual "here," versus a world of separate objects "out there." When we are ready, when we dare to drop that belief and take a look and believe what we see, not what we have been told by so-called "others," the true vision of Who We Really Are opens.

So I say, have the courage to look back. See the Aware Void at the core of your being. Keep noticing it whenever you can. See that it is No-thing and is wide awake and is what you are, right where you are. The rest will eventually come.

Okay, but I want to know how that chair is here and is, as you say, what I am. That seems so absurd that it makes me doubt everything you're telling me.

Well, you could start by asking science. Where does science tell you that you see anything? Here, where you are, right? Do you experience that chair over there, or do you experience it right where you are, at the terminus of the visual process that science claims is where anything is seen. Look into that, then look at that very terminus you are looking out of. Don't let distance hoodwink you into believing the chair — or anything perceived — is "over there." It is where you see it, which is where you are. ...But again, this will come. And when it does it will be obvious that the Awareness you can actually see at your core is also capacity for the world. In fact, a better name for it might be Aware Capacity. This is What You Are — Aware Capacity for the world!

Some of what you're saying makes sense. You know, I get these little "Aha!" moments, like all of a sudden I get it! And then the next second I'm more confused than ever. But whatever happened to what we started with — having everything and where we'd put it? That's what began all this.

You are Aware Capacity for the world, for everything. How much more could you have it! The world and everything in it is inside you. If you look back at where you think (!) you have a head and see only awake emptiness, you may see that this emptiness is also filled with the scene, that at this very moment, where you are, you are Capacity for anything and everything. That pencil on the desk, that chair, that building, those mountains and the distant horizon and every thought and feeling and memory and expectation and image you have, are inside the Aware Capacity that you are.

So they are not "over there" as you have been taught. They are Here where you are. You are Room for them. You "have" them all. You couldn't be more intimate with them. In fact, they are What You Are, and only appearing as "other." There is no separation, no distance, nothing apart from the complete Subjectivity that you are.

There's nowhere to go after that. That's the end, isn't it?

For now.

And the game continues.

Yes, that too. You could call that the "practice," playing the game and playing it well and knowing that every now-moment is What You Are. It's the movement of the universe, and you are the universe. It's love in apparent action. Many have said it's sacred. It's also lovely beyond compare, don't you agree?

I'm trying.

PART THREE

THE MAN IN THE OTHER BATHROOM

Since everything is but an apparition
Perfect in being what it is
Having nothing to do with good or bad,
Acceptance or rejection,
You might as well burst out laughing!"

--Longchenpa, from
The Treasury of the Basic Space of Phenomena

RELEASE

To my astonishment, I was released from prison this year on a technicality after serving 35 years on the wrong law governing my sentence. It happened quickly, and directly from the courtroom (and county jail) at 8:30 on a wintry evening dressed in nothing more than jail clothes: T-shirt, sweatpants, and sneakers. Fortunately, my attorney, the same attorney who had worked tirelessly on my case for 6 years for no fee, showed up in her car to drive me to a friend's house, an ex-con I knew who had done more time than I had, the two of us often together in the same prison facility.

I can say today and will always say that, other than my LSD trips in the early 1960s, the ride from the jail in my attorney's car was the most surreal experience I have known. The car, unlike prison vans and buses, sat low to the ground and seemed to be speeding beyond all limits despite registering 35 on the speedometer. I found myself bracing as if it were a rocket, landing nose first, a spaceship that had arrived on an alien planet where nothing was familiar, not the buildings, not the signs, not the oddly dressed creatures on the sidewalks. At a stop light, a man wearing black with a flashing red light pinned to the back of his jacket flew across in front of us on a skateboard, and moments later the white lines of a freeway penetrated my stare while more spaceships hovered around us, humming above the roadway.

I slept that night in a real bed with a soft pillow. I slept better than I had in longer than I could remember, and when I awoke in the morning my friend led me to the kitchen and sat me in front of a cup of real coffee and real eggs (over easy) with three slices of something I hadn't tasted in a very long time — bacon! We chatted briefly, and he pointed at the window and the expansive view of the back yard and beyond. There were deer, at least a dozen of them, the youngsters cavorting on the frozen hill behind the yard. The trees and bushes were bare, but it could have been the lushest rainforest this side of the Amazon and it wouldn't have impressed as much as that cold and woody back yard of that 1950sstyle house set in a neighborhood of the same, an overgrown creek running wild just past the fence.

I called a friend I hadn't seen in a decade since he'd left prison. I thought he dropped the phone when he realized I was free. He drove 30 minutes from his house, picked me up and drove me to a nearby park. We strolled on a path down an incline to a brook where there were ducks paddling close to the bank, carving circles in the icy water. I watched them as they watched me—open, contented—and then suddenly and unexpectedly I burst into tears, overwhelmed with the beauty, the awareness of awareness brimming with more love and splendor than I could contain, all at once. When I recovered, we stood in silence for a while, then continued along the path and back to the car, that blissful vision imprinted forever in my memory.

Safeway was a magic show of gleaming plastic and unrecognizable food, aisles beckoning with garish color and promises no one could keep. Vegetables, fruits, nuts, even boxed goods were "organic," yet nothing seemed real. I marveled at the "rain" drizzling down over the fresh produce, the canned thunder to let one know it was coming. There were entire sections of prepared foods, bakery products, walls of dairy behind glass panels, processed and packaged meats, fish laid bare on ice as if fresh. What could I possibly do with it? I had no idea how to cook; I had been eating a limited menu of prison food, most of it canned or frozen and all of it low-grade, for over 35 years, served directly to me on thick plastic slop trays with reusable sporks. If it weren't now for my friend, how and what would I eat, how would I do anything? For with freedom comes choice and the responsibility to know more than survival at the mercy of the rigid structure of prison. I had forgotten what fresh food looked like, and had never seen such a confusing array of packaging. How would I cook it? What were the proper portions, what went together, how much did it cost, how would I afford even the most basic of goods? Order online? — I had never even seen a laptop or a cellphone, except on TV; when I went to prison, typewriters were still common. The names Microsoft and Apple were relatively unknown back then, the technology of personal computers in its most primitive stage. How would I handle the diverse explosion of information with the keyboard chops of a five-year-old?

At the check-out counter I was lost. Had it not been for my friend and his sister, I might have backed away and left with nothing. Paying in cash seemed not an option. Because I was released directly from court and not from the prison itself, I did not receive my $100 "gate" money in the form of a temporary debit card; instead I relied on the generosity of friends for clothing and cash, at least until I could qualify for food stamps or some other assistance before securing a job — but who would hire a nearly eighty-year-old felon with little real-world experience and no knowledge of today's technology?

As it happened, I needn't have been concerned. I knew beforehand that everything I needed was right in front of me, or rather, already within me. If it wasn't, I didn't need it. It was that simple, and as the answer to all my questions about the past or the future, it was simply the only answer for the present moment, or any moment.

Every possible article of clothing I could want, winter or summer, was handed to me. Checks arrived in the mail. My first month's rent was paid for by a grant from a senior citizens group in the city where I settled. Because of my poor balance and a need for transportation, money for an adult tricycle showed up. Bus passes, food banks, Medicaid, a local pension of sorts, all appeared as if by magic, right on time. I have no so-called "real world" explanation for such arrivals, and I would never claim that karma or cause and effect are operative. Like everyone else, often without realizing it, I have fabricated these stories of individual experience, stories which in the end turn out to be lame accounts for what is undoubtedly The One with no parts, no separation, no exceptions. I have made up the stories of "life as it is," and in so doing have made up a world of left and right and up and down, of good and bad and right and wrong and all the multifaceted colors that comprise the drama of life and death. And the world-story rolls on, issuing forth on the wheels of the farmer's creed: "What ye sow, so shall ye reap." What more could our "practice" consist of but to See Who We Really Are and act from THAT, as THAT, sowing and reaping the gift of the Source, ever mindful of and ever grateful for this magnificent illusion of change?

The bird-feeder hanging from the eave outside the kitchen window is crowded with sparrows, and a fat squirrel has found my donation of an acorn squash I didn't want. This old house probably has more spiders than St. Louis has people, and I love how they go about their business as I go about mine. The forecast today is for sun and warmer temperatures the next three days, so it's time to roll out the trike and pedal this upside-down body absolutely nowhere, marveling at what arrives and disappears into the stillness of this Awake Void, aware that the Void and what arrives are one and the same, Pure Subjectivity. Could this interplay of Who I Really Am disguised as who I am not be more hilarious? More mysterious? More mind-blowing? More that which truly is?

Morning light welcomes me, and this day, like every day, I rise with the excitement of a kid making his first visit to Disneyworld, despite the fact that I have six medical appointments in the next four days for age-related ailments that have mostly been ignored. This body ages, but thank God I don't. This body, desiccated, prune-like, held together with fabricated parts of titanium and plastic, wobbly and unsure of step, now serves me like it never has, for it has never been clearer that I'm not a resident of it, but that it's a resident of Me, as are all things, all time, all space. It's an odd love affair of the apparent and non-apparent, odd because there are not two here, yet a love affair just the same. Void/Form. Emptiness/Fullness. Never different, never apart, always in love.

So I'm up and ready for my Magic Mountain day, today for the excising of skin cancer and a pressure check for glaucoma. It's chilly this morning, but the sky is clear and ultra-bright. I must remember to get air in my trike tires, and maybe a coffee on the way, cream, no sugar, an out-of-the-way place I've never been to before.

BARE NAKED AWARENESS

"In the absence of that which you are not,
that which you are . . . is not."
—Neale Donald Walsch

As "God" assured us in the *Conversations With God* books by Neale Donald Walsch, you are making up the story of your life, of life in general, of everything. Without the story, there is simply bare naked awareness that cannot be experienced because it is what you are and you are not separate from it to experience it. There is truly no meaning to life except the meaning you assign to it, which in turn is the greatest possible gift of freedom and the foundation of all gratitude, sometimes called "grace."

So the question is: How do you experience Who You Really Are when there is no "you" to experience it? And the answer is: That which You manifests as, which happens to be anything and everything, is that which You experience! Therefore, everything that appears—all scenes, all things, all beings—all of which appear both in and as Who You Really are, are what you experience. So the only thing you can ever experience is Who You Really Are! In other words, Pure Subjectivity experiences only Itself because all there is, is Pure Subjectivity. There is nothing else. That is, there is nothing outside or separate from Pure Subjectivity.

So again, how does Oneness see Itself? Contrary to what one might think, seeing Who You Really are turns out to be the easiest thing possible. Why? Because wherever you look, there you are! Meister Eckhart said it this way in the 14th Century: "The eye through which I see God is the same eye through which God sees me; my eye and God's eye are one eye, one seeing, one knowing, one love."

Or do what so many have done over the years since Douglas Harding came up with the easy and direct (and incredibly simple) awareness exercises he termed "experiments." Simply point at where you believe you have a face, but drop the belief that you have a face. Then look at what your finger is pointing at. What I then see here is space, no-thing, but not simply nothing-at-all (as in the opposite of something) because it is a no-thing that is aware, and furthermore, aware that it is aware. What you see, if only momentarily, is God, and furthermore, it is God seeing Himself, the very same God that Meister Eckhart spoke of in the 14th Century. And you can do so anytime you want (which is always Now) and anywhere you want (which is always Here), whatever your mood or situation, which of course is Who You Really Are appearing as a mood or situation!

So pick any story. Pick whatever suits your fancy and pretend you're in it. You might as well, you're doing it anyway, right now. So why not do it consciously? You're an actor in a marvelous play scripted by Yourself! And as Krishna advised Arjuna in the *Bhagavad Gita*, play the part like any good actor would, to the best of your ability. Win the Oscar as the best rendition of "yourself," the actor-self you are moment by moment creating in (and as) Who You Really Are—Bare Naked Awareness—which in turn is appearing as "you," having "a life." There is no separate one and no separate thing else. There is only Pure Subjectivity (and not even that).

By the way, the play, this life-manifestation, is an absolute miracle. It is pure joy. Its essence is Awareness, God, Who You Really Are. Above all, it is Love. Pay it forward.

STORIES OF ONENESS

Recently I was asked to talk to a group of ex-cons about Oneness, a subject I imagined they would have little interest in. I began with a measure of trepidation, facing, as it were, several men in various states of slouch, and when I introduced myself and said:

"So, can you tell me, what is it that you need to be you?"—there followed a long pause, pregnant with looks of disbelief, and then finally the snide remarks I was expecting:

"A six-pack of Bud," one man said. "Yeah, a girlfriend who doesn't nag me about where I've been," said another, guffawing.

"I need this body," I said, pointing to my chest. "And of course I need all the parts that make up this body, such as my torso, arms, hands, legs, and feet, and there's also my internal organs: heart, liver, lungs, kidneys, guts, plus my circulatory and nervous systems. And, I imagine you need the same. So what else? What more do you need to be you?"

Another pause, and then finally an answer. "What those parts are made of," a man said. "Cells."

"Yes," I said. "And cells are made of molecules and molecules are made of atoms, and so on down to particles and quarks. So what you need is an incredible cast of characters, literally zillions and zillions of them, from your body as a whole to your internal organs and the cells that comprise them and on down to the countless molecules, atoms, and particles that in turn make up those cells, all of which function as one unit under the name you call yourself. What else do you need?"

"Things outside yourself," another man said. "Like other people. Food. Water."

"Yes. You need the things we say are 'outside' your body. You need humans and their farms and markets and distribution centers and all that goes into keeping us alive. But this just doesn't happen by itself."

"We need nature," he said.

"Yes, we need the earth, its atmosphere and biosphere. We need air and rivers and oceans and animals and insects and plants. We need all of that. And the sun, the solar system, other planets, gravity. Where would be without gravity? Or the galaxy? You need all of those things, all in perfect working order. How long would you last if the sun went out? Where would you be if there were no galaxy, no universe?"

The room seemed less hostile. At least those who had spoken were now sitting up. I said, "You can't rightfully say 'me' without including all of that—quarks to galaxy and beyond—because you need every single bit of it to be 'you' sitting in this room right now. So if you think of yourself as a separate individual who is alone and unique and completely one-off, is that really true? The next time you flaunt your ego thinking that what you see in the mirror is a singular and special 'you,' you might want to think about what you're leaving out. And that includes other people, not to mention absolutely everything else."

No one said a word, so I continued.

"Here's another way to look at it," I said. "I'll paraphrase this from a chapter in a book written by a man who changed my outlook to what is now an inlook, which in turn changed my attitude and everything else in the world. It goes like this:

"Let's say you're driving on the interstate and you decide to pull off at the next exit and get a cup of coffee. You find a booth and notice on the menu that a cup of coffee costs $3.20, which seems like an outrageous price for a lousy cup of coffee, but where else are you going to get one? The waitress takes your order, despite your grumbling about the cost, and then as she's walking away you begin to wonder how she ended up here working in this restaurant out in the middle of nowhere. All the thousands of possibilities that must have existed for her to be anywhere else right now, yet here she is in this place. Maybe she grew up on a farm around here, maybe her husband is from some town nearby, maybe she wanted her kids to go to a rural school—there could easily be a million little events and choices in her life that put her in this restaurant at this moment retrieving your cup of coffee.

"And then you think about the owner and all the responsibilities he has, the bills he pays, the daily burden of running this restaurant that is providing you with your coffee. And the building itself—all the materials that went into it, the construction company that built it and all their personnel, the designers and blueprints, the electrical, plumbing, and landscaping companies, all contributing to your immediate need, and each with their own million events and choices that had to be perfectly aligned so as to be essential to your present experience.

"But let's not forget the coffee maker and everything it took to design and manufacture and market it, and all the people involved there, and of course the coffee itself—follow that back to the delivery truck and the driver and the distributer, and then to the company that imports the beans and grinds and packages the coffee. And then there's the cargo ship and the shipping company that brings the beans from, say, Columbia, and the materials and construction of the ship itself, and the hundreds, perhaps thousands, of people involved going all the way back to the mining of the raw materials needed to build it. Then there is the coffee plantation and the owners and managers and workers, and of course the plants that produce the beans and the fertile soil they grow in and just the right amount of water needed, and we can't leave out the land, the country, the continent, the earth itself and its atmosphere, the sun and solar system, the galaxy, the universe as a whole. When you come down to it, it really is mind-boggling to consider all that was involved to produce that precious cup of coffee just for you at this very moment in this very place. And you got all that for the incredible deal of only $3.20! "As they used to say in my favorite deli in New York: 'So what's not to love?'"

I turned to the whiteboard and drew several concentric circles, labeling the space inside the inner circle "Feeling," the space within the next circle "Tasting," the space within the next "Touching," the next "Smelling," then "Hearing," then "Seeing," and finally, outside all the circles and reaching to the edge of the board, "Thinking/ Visualizing."

To the group I said, "My question is, why do you normally consider that your body ends at the edge of the inside third ring? Why do the experiences of feeling, tasting, and touching strike you as happening inside the boundary of your body, while smelling, hearing, and seeing are mostly linked to things outside your body? And of course thinking and visualizing may run from quarks and particles to the farthest reaches of the universe and beyond, and include every possible fantastic variation. The point is, if you investigate, if you look inside yourself and tell the truth about how you really perceive anything, I think you'll agree that all perceptions are experienced inside. All that you experience via your senses happens right where you are, moment by moment, and that includes everything you see, hear, smell, touch, taste, feel, and think. The key word here is experience. Your experience can't happen anywhere but right where you are, right at the moment you experience it. It is not experienced somewhere else because you are not somewhere else, other than where you are! Any past experience you remember is a thought and not the actual experience, and the same is true of any imagined future experience.

So not only can any actual experience happen right *where* you are but it can only happen right *when* you are, in the exact moment it happens, which we know as 'Now.' In short, experience is only 'Here' and only 'Now.' "This leads me to the next question: How do you even know there is a 'somewhere else?' Considering that everything you experience you experience where you are, you could just as easily conclude that there is no outside world, despite what science says about how we as assumed objects relate with other assumed objects, a process that really only describes how objects connect and says nothing about how we actually experience anything. Really, your own experiential evidence should be the determining factor. I think it's clear, based on my own present experience and not on what anyone else tells me to believe, that everything I experience I experience here, inside. That awareness of anything, no matter what it is, happens where I am, not 'over there,' including the experience of thoughts about so-called 'other' wheres or whens, or thoughts of all manner of things—people, places, and objects—the things that thoughts are attached to. And where is this 'awareness'? I don't know about you, but I have never seen someone else's awareness. In fact, I have never seen awareness anywhere else. I see it only here, where I am. Actually, it is so 'where I am' that I cannot distinguish between 'it' and 'I.' All of the terms I have been using are interchangeable: 'I,' 'Here,' 'Experience,' and 'Awareness.' Moreover, it is impossible to conclude from this that there is anything separate from anything else, that there exists any sort of 'duality.' It is all inside. It is all within experience. In fact, it is experience—there is nothing other than experience—and that's about as close as we can get to Oneness other than to say that there is nothing anywhere except perhaps for the appearance or the illusion of a space/time universe of separate parts, a world we make up, appearing inside awareness. An elaborate dream, if you will."

I waited, and said, "How are we doing with this?"

"Deep," I heard, and while most remained slumped in their chairs, the same few who had spoken seemed interested.

"If you follow nature or science shows on TV or in magazines, almost invariably these days you hear the word 'interconnectedness' or 'interdependence.' Mostly there will be an example of how two species benefit each other, how plants and insects, for instance, form a workable bargain of protection and sustenance, and there may be illustrations of the overall interdependence of a rainforest or the oceans. Actually, these are not separate and solitary cases of oneness; rather, they speak of the entirety of the universe as a whole. It—we—are not separate parts. That is to say, we are not "we." "We" are "I."

"Like the butterfly effect," one man blurted out. "A butterfly flapping its wings in the Amazon causes a thunderstorm in Iowa."

"I don't believe that stuff," another man added.

I said, "Here's a quote from an astronaut/scientist on a recent National Geographic show*: 'There is absolutely nothing on one side of the planet that is not connected to something on the other side of the planet.'" To that I added, "The connection may not be as dramatic as the butterfly image, but nevertheless there is a connection, whether or not it is obvious."
"So what's this got to do with us?"

"A lot," I said. "When we think we're separate, when we do what we do for 'number one' with the attitude that 'I'm gettin' mine and I'm gettin' it first!', we not only create problems for everyone around us, we end up where we've all ended up—in prison. And that isn't the half of it."

I said, "There's an ancient Hindu metaphor called Indra's Net which illuminates this principle well. Picture the universe as a gigantic net, and where each of the strands meet, there is a jewel. Each of these jewels reflects all the other jewels of the net, and every jewel represents, say, an object or a form of life. If you doubt that all the jewels are intimately interconnected, place a dot on one jewel, and because the jewels all reflect each other, they will all immediately display a dot. Applying that to human beings, when one jewel, say, acts selfishly or harms another, then all the other jewels are affected. You have only to turn on the nightly news to see the situation the world presently finds itself in, and to bring that same metaphor to a personal level, you can see how when you so much as think selfishly, how the world will respond to you. It's the Farmer's Creed: 'What ye sow, so shall ye reap,' and there we were in prison, reaping what we had sown. That, in a nutshell, is the action of Oneness, the principle of interrelatedness that is so intimate as to defy any notion of intrinsic individuality or separateness. 'We' are 'I.'"

"Yeah, but what if someone else started the bad stuff and others have been reaping it ever since. That's the way it's been for me, and I don't see no change coming."

"The point is," I said, "there isn't anyone else doing anything because there's only Oneness. So it's up to you to be the One, and to act accordingly. When you love others, you are loving yourself because all there is, is you, as One. The mirroring effect of the jewels represents not zillions of individual jewels reflecting each other; rather, each jewel is every other jewel. I used the word 'intimate' when describing interrelatedness, but really, there are not two to be so. When you have two mirrors perfectly mirroring each other, are there then still two mirrors? On the surface, from a source outside the mirrors (which is impossible in the metaphor of Indra's Net, and in fact, is impossible in reality, as the principle of Hadron's Bootstrap in quantum physics points out), the answer may be 'yes,' but within the mirror images, there is no longer an answer because the question is no longer a question.

"I think we all know the result of not acting accordingly, of not recognizing Oneness. When we believe we are all separate beings living in a world of separate parts, there soon appears confrontation, brought on by our need to be happy, to make a living, to find our way in this labyrinth we call 'a life.'

And invariably we assign responsibility, especially for the so-called 'bad' deeds, to those we think of as "others." Too often we do this so as to make it easier for ourselves; we feel better about ourselves when we can assign blame to someone else. And my belief is that the reason we feel bad about ourselves to begin with is because we bought into the lie of separateness when we were young and now find ourselves clueless about the One Source that we really are. In a word, we're stuck, and we don't even know it, and blame becomes the daily norm, gossip the common exchange, confrontation the lifestyle. You know as well as I do. In prison we saw this every day. Despite the few acts of charity, it was mostly dog-eat-dog, and although the sentiment may be socially cleaner on the outside, it's basically the same game: 'Do unto me as I do unto me.'"

"So what can we do? Seems to me, we're the last people who could do anything about it."

"No, I don't believe that," I said. "We may be the very ones to be the One we truly are. We ended up in prison because of what we did. As prisoners, our deeds were in our face every hour of every day. We were in our self-made pit, removed from the game, and that might have been more valuable than we realize. Byron Katie once said that she loved doing The Work (her method of opening to the Source) in prisons because prisoners were on the edge; they would go to great lengths, even kill their own children, to find God. So maybe we are perfectly qualified; maybe we've lashed out against the norm for reasons we haven't yet considered. Most of us were backed into the worst of corners and thought that more of what we lacked—sex, drugs, and rock and roll—was the cure for our pain. Eventually we realize that the old methods don't work, and to address the still-present yearning inside, we realize we can no longer stand on our old beliefs, while the majority of folks go about their separate business in their separate neighborhoods never considering who they really are nor changing what they have become comfortable with, despite the fact that they are living a lie."

"Yeah, but how?" the same man said. "You don't just flip a switch and you're changed."

"So maybe just think about what was said today. Here's an image that helped me remember early on. I got it from a book by Alan Watts on eastern wisdom: Picture a ship sailing across the ocean. Naturally it creates a wake behind it, like all ships do, right? So the ship causes the wake, or we can say the ship is 'responsible' for the wake. Now, you are the ship, and you are responsible for your wake. Your choices, your actions, cause the result of those actions. But when you blame someone else, what you're saying is that the wake is causing the ship. 'Someone else (the wake) started this crap, and I (the ship) am paying for it.' So every time you want to blame someone (or something) for how you are doing or how you are feeling, remember that you've lost control of the ship, that as captain of yourself you have turned your power and authority over to someone else, and in so doing you are at the mercy of people or things you mistakenly believe are separate from yourself. In effect, you are saying that the wake is responsible for the ship. That's how absurd it is to blame, and because we do this so often, it's a great reminder that we have forgotten the Oneness that is our true nature.

"So I say, it's a start. Or go to the library, read science books and magazines, read Eastern spirituality, try meditation and yoga, ask questions. Get interested in who or what you really are. Why come to the end of your life never having looked, never knowing or caring about what you are or what this universe is. I say do whatever it takes, be aware of what presents itself to you, what resonates. If you relax your mind, something will come along. Simply don't prevent it. Examine your beliefs. Be open to anything that shows up. It will respond."

It was time to leave, and for a brief moment I was certain that no one in the room had understood, despite the few who had participated. But then the truth arrived, and did so on the wings of the bodhisattva vow: "A bodhisattva vows not to take enlightenment until all others are enlightened" (even though a bodhisattva knows quite well that there are no others).

And so I looked back at what I was looking out of, here where I see no face, no head, only awareness—empty, pure, singular, first-person-present-tense awareness, which I saw, literally saw, nowhere else in the universe, and I knew in that momentary vision of Oneness that everyone had both spoken and heard every word and that all was perfectly timed and perfectly executed for the only audience, that of Oneness.

And I left the way I entered, through the door.

Or rather, here in the stillness of awareness, I watched as the door approached and grew larger, then vanished into this vast and empty awareness that I am.

SO WHAT'S NOT TO LOVE?

In the last chapter I mentioned a road trip and stopping for a cup of coffee at an inn. It was hopefully a workable example of the principle of Oneness, how everything is interconnected in an intricate web of relationships in such a way as to defy the notion of separate parts, or of any parts. But isn't it also a fine example of what we know as Grace, the freely given gift of a fully alive and perfectly functioning universe by, as, and for Who We Really Are, this wide awake Single Eye, this conscious empty Capacity for everything that is found only right here and right now?

To say that Seeing Who You Really Are—actually looking back at what you are looking out of and rediscovering the boundless awake emptiness at the heart of the world—to say that this Beatific Vision can engender gratitude is an understatement of the grandest proportions. I don't know why. The Vision itself is neutral. After all, it is empty, is not an object, has no qualities, no boundaries, altogether defies description and cannot be compared to anything whatsoever. It is pure Subjectivity and is therefore beyond thinking and feeling which are "downstream" of it, and yet gratitude radiates from it freely.

The Benedictine monk David Steindl-Rast said: "Everything is a gift. The degree to which we are awake to this truth is a measure of our gratefulness, and gratefulness is a measure of our aliveness."

He didn't say that good things are gifts and bad things are not. He said that everything is a gift.

Seeing that you are empty, seeing that you are pure awareness, is to enter the second step of the Buddha's formula: 1.) First there are mountains and rivers (ordinary, or relative seeing); 2.) Then there are no mountains and rivers (seeing Who You Are as empty awareness); 3.) Then once again there are mountains and rivers (seen as an aspect of Who You Are).

It is the second step that is the entrance to wisdom (and a trap if you remain there), but it is the final step that is true awakening, and it is available if you look, if you drop what you have learned as a child from others (parents, teachers, friends, all of whom were never where you are at the source), and instead go on present evidence, on what you and you alone actually see.

Try this (and reading about it will do nothing; one must actually do it): First, point at where you think (!) you have a face and look in the direction your finger is pointing. In other words, look back at what you are looking out of. See—on present evidence—that you have no face, that indeed in place of a head there appears the world (the scene, whatever is viewed at that moment). Notice that the empty awareness is open for the world, that there is no boundary, no dividing line between the one and the other.

Notice also that the world easily fits within this awareness that you are, that awareness is boundless and infinitely vast and that all scenes, no matter what, easily fit within it, and that it has always been this way. Awareness and the world are always one, right where you are when you are, and that includes whatever thoughts and feelings that are attached to the scene, be that scene current, or be it memories or expectations attached to visualizations. The world is awareness, and awareness is the world.

This is the recognition of Oneness. There cannot be a second, never has been and never will be. Seeing this is experiencing this, being this. It is the recognition of Who You Really Are. It is grace, in that everything is your own gift to yourself. There is no benefactor and no recipient other than You, and from this recognition springs gratitude, and from gratitude, joy, the sort of joy that has nothing to do with having gotten what you want or having something wonderful happen. This is the experiential apprehension of Indra's Net, the God-Hologram. This is seeing Awake No-thing here filled to the brim with all that you once mistakenly thought was "out there." This is Void and Form as one, Awake Nothing appearing as the scene and the scene appearing as a manifestation of Awake No-thing, as One.

It may seem odd, therefore, that almost every day I recite what I am grateful for, as if there are two, me and whatever or whomever it is I happen to include. I do this out loud. The list includes friends, events, places, and things, but inevitably it leads to a gratitude that cannot be accounted for by people and things. I end it by simply saying, "I am grateful for THIS!"

Why do I recite what I am grateful for? Because I find that giving thanks is the natural result of seeing Who I Am. Here, THIS, is magical. That people and things appear at all is profoundly astonishing. There could be, and perhaps should be, simply nothing, no space or time or matter, no universe at all. But that THIS, this Awakeness, this Empty Consciousness, this Boundless Eye that both simultaneously creates and is capacity for a universe of everything—and is unquestionably present as Who I AM—this truly is the Great Mystery, one that revels in its creation and erupts in gratitude and veneration. Here, where the end of the list is reached, gratitude cannot be distinguished from Love.

And as David Steindl-Rast made clear, everything is a gift. Oneness reveals this. The universe itself is a gift—it is what you are—and you are the giver, the gift, and the receiver. There are no separate parts. Everything is freely given and freely received. There is no quid pro quo exchange. There are no debts, no requirements to respond in like kind. "We" who are not "we" merely function as THIS—Awakening—passing it forward, knowing that everything appearing, that which is referred to in Zen as "the ten thousand things," is THIS, What I Really Am. We may think that receiving a gift dictates that we respond in some way, but this is false thinking based on the premise that we are intrinsically separate beings living in a world of separate parts "out there." In reality, "we" are this one Awake Space appearing as everything, and seeing this, who could there be to be a benefactor or beneficiary, who could be the giver and who the receiver, and of what?

And so we act our part in this great drama of love; we pass it forward. We are the agents of gratitude, the jewels of Indra's Net reflecting all the other jewels, each one the manifestation of a universe of infinite gifts. We receive, and we give. We give, and we receive, and never do we owe. We simply pass it on, and this, ultimately, is Who You Are, passing to Yourself. As David Steindl-Rast also said, "As I express my gratitude, I become more deeply aware of it. And the greater my awareness, the greater my need to express it. What happens here is a spiraling ascent, a process of growth in ever expanding circles around a steady center."

In the mornings when I open the drapes in my room, I see a flood of green, a spacious back yard overgrown and bursting with tall grass, wildly unkempt bushes, and trees with leaves so numerous the neighboring houses have disappeared. There are tunnels of overhanging foliage, and hardly a foot of the back fence is visible. Beyond, the creek murmurs, winding nearly unseen through a riot of weeds on its bank.

Although I began my practice of gratitude in prison several years ago, in these several months since my release I am experiencing gratitude in a new and inspiring way. These mornings are sometimes overwhelmingly beautiful, and gratitude brings tears.

Stepping outside, the awe of placing my hand on the trunk of a tree, something I hadn't done in 35 years, the scent of wildflowers from the hill beyond the creek, my slippers wet with dew, this dazzling scene in the morning sun immediately replacing me — how could this be paid forward? How can anything be paid forward?

My only answer is: by Seeing. Seeing Who I Really Am pays

everything forward, and to Itself. Seeing provides the urge to "do" what we "are," and to choose what we See. Gratitude is so deeply linked to Who I Really Am that at times I can no longer distinguish between the two. And of all the endless gifts presented moment by moment, the fact that they appear here not only for but as Aware Presence—this is the Final Gift, right where I am. THIS is where it begins and ends, where it all originates and never left.

And for all the men I knew in prison, and for all the men and women in prison everywhere, here is David Steindl-Rast again:

"If you're grateful, you're not fearful, and if you're not fearful, you're not violent. If you're grateful, you act out of a sense of enough and not a sense of scarcity, and you're willing to share. If you are grateful, you are enjoying the differences between people, and you are respectful to everybody, and that changes this power pyramid under which we live."

TWO-WAY SEEING

"Above all, this meditation, Janus-like, faces both ways.
Simultaneously looking in at the Seer and out at the seen, it takes in and
makes sense of the seen because it puts No-thing in its way — and gives
priority to this No-thing. Seek the 1st person and the 3rd shall be added.
Seek the 3rd, and even that shall be taken away."
—Douglas Harding

With one hand, point back at what you are looking out of, at where you thought you had a face, and notice there is nothing there but empty space, awake to its own emptiness. With the other hand held next to the first, point out at the scene.

You are now simultaneously looking in at empty awareness and out at the scene in front of you. Notice that there is no dividing line between the empty awareness and the scene, the nothing and the something. They are united, right here where you are.

This is Oneness, void and form as void/form, what you truly are. Another way to say it: As Source (pure awareness, empty of all objectivity), you are void appearing as form. You are empty awareness manifesting as the changing scene.

They are not different. They have never been different.

You are the absence of time, always now, manifesting as passing time, appearing as the "past" (thoughts and memories), the "present" (which is already the past by the time you register it), and the future (expectations and imagination), all of which happen in awareness now.

There is no time other than the immediate presence of awareness (always now), and there is no space other than that same awareness in which every scene appears and disappears (always here). This coming and going is true of your flesh body, your thoughts, your feelings, and ultimately the universe — anything and everything appears in and as awareness. All are objects appearing inside What You Really Are, which has been called Pure Subjectivity, spaceless and timeless and fully aware, aware even of being aware. It is simply a matter of coming home to what you already are. You've been away, living "out there," pretending to be someone you're not, someone you thought you were, but it was never true. You are not the body and not the mind. The body and mind happen inside the timeless and spaceless Awareness, the Consciousness that you truly are.

THE FOOL

The Fool is not who you think you are.

The Fool is not who you look like to other people from where they are, "over there."

The Fool is not what you see in the mirror; it too is "over there."

The Fool is at no distance from where you are, right where you are.

The Fool is not an object, not an image, not an appearance.

The Fool turns who you think you are inside-out and upside down.

The Fool is no one, no thing, and no thought.

All those appear inside the Fool, by and as the Fool.

The Fool simultaneously creates and experiences the illusion of space and time, yet occupies neither.

The Fool is anywhere imaginable, yet never moves.

The Fool is always Here, which is nowhere, no matter where.

The Fool is always Now, which is nowhen, no matter when.

The Fool is timeless, prior to time.

The Fool cannot be named, yet manifests as anything and everything.

The Fool is empty, yet is not nothing.

The Fool is awake, aware, yet cannot know what it is because it is the knowing of what is known.

The Fool is pure subjectivity.

The Fool may be said to be One in that there are no other Fools, but the Fool is not singular either.

The Fool was never born and can never die.

YOU are the Fool. Be THAT. You might as well. You cannot not be THAT!

PROBLEMS, PROBLEMS

"All problems have but one universal solution."
—*Anandamayi Ma*

So what could be the "problem?" Nearly every day I run into something called a problem, then come to my senses and have to smile. How could I possibly call something a "problem?" Who is this so-called "me" that thinks there's a problem? Am I stuck in the small scheme of things? Are we really separate individuals briefly existing in an indifferent universe too vast to comprehend? Am I no more than a zeptosecond of meaningless dust confronting one problem after another until my demise?

Or am I what I actually see here at my core: this boundless, awake Emptiness, this capacious creator of all things, all time and space? Which is it—that which I see—the picture worth a thousand words—or that which I think? Is it available right now when I reverse my attention and look at what I am looking out of, or is it something I learned as a child and have repeated ad infinitum, the lie of duality handed down from the generations, the "original sin" of separation?

There aren't any so-called problems, of course. They are illusions, part of the game of what we call "life." Let's first see them for what they are: negative thoughts attached to scenes. And properly understood, let's then realize that they are gifts, reminders of what we are not, and then by contrast, of what we truly are, which is No-thing Here and Now, and never some-thing there and then. Thank God for problems, I say, and the tip-off is the feelings they bring with them, alarms that tell me that I've lost the center, that I'm mired in thoughts attached to the things of this world. There are days when I seem to have more than my share of them, and then, often in retrospect, I marvel at the intelligence of this Empty Awareness that came up with this ingenious method of coming Home. It's an astonishing bargain, and it never fails to bring wonder accompanied by laughter—that Who I Really Am could create Itself posing as who I am not for the purpose of recognizing Who I Really Am! And the beauty and genius of the Headless Way is that this recognition is so vividly confirmed by the senses, so "on display" merely by looking to see, no matter the situation or mood. Look back, and notice Space here, world there. Which am I attending to? Or am I attending to both?—Space here filled with the world, as One? Have I not created this marvelous union of Self appearing as other, yet seeing only One (and not even that!)? Are you not, as the One (and anyone can say this) living in a world of only Yourself? How could it be otherwise?

But wait, here it comes again, the movie of my life, filled with all sorts of characters, the usual twists and turns and unscheduled arrivals, scenes of laughter and joy and the occasional adventure, and of course, the problems, some without apparent solutions.

Which reminds me of a passage in the Bible: "Seek ye first the kingdom of God, and all shall be added unto you." Caught by the movie, or worse, caught in the movie and thinking I'm one of the characters (the leading man, of course), I am seeking pleasure and avoiding pain. There is no way out of this lifetime seesaw—without it there'd be no world—and as time passes, I find myself more and more on the downside because of old age.

Unless, of course, I turn my attention around 180 degrees and first look Here, then see that There has been added into the bargain, appearing inside Me. Here—Awareness. There—the "ten thousand things." And every one of them appears inside this Awareness that I am. It was in this manner when I was in prison that I discovered I wasn't in prison—prison was in Me. And in the same way, I now see that this keyboard and monitor and the words on this screen are inside Me, as well as any and all thoughts that are attached to this scene. Because this has been my experience in the past every time I've looked, I expect it will be the same in the future when I look (although both the memory and the expectation are Here/Now). Because others say it is the same for them when they look, I am warmed by the connection, especially knowing that there are no "others," nor any such monstrosity as "multiple awarenesses." There is only Awareness, and it is no-thing, and it is What We Are.

And so I look down and see this headless aging body and feel the accumulating aches, and even marvel at how wobbly and forgetful I've become these past few months. And I notice the thoughts swirling around these daily infirmities that arise: the twinge in the knee, the pain in the chest that is probably indigestion, the worry about a hip replacement that twice has dislocated, the neuropathy in my legs, emphysema, skin cancer, and all the other signs of advancing decrepitude.

And yet, looking back and seeing this Infinite Void that I am that welcomes these ills, I see the rightness of things going wrong. And I see this inside Who I Am, at once the Creator and Experiencer of Myself. And I know beyond a doubt that I am unborn and undying and timelessly healthy as No-thing, prior to space and time and the stories I have fashioned, including this one about a mortal body and mind.

How can I not be grateful for such a gift? Not just for the body and this long life but for the story as well — and I make no excuses for the darkness I perpetrated or the laws I broke for so long. It is a case of dying to the sins of the past and being reborn to the purity of the present. It is the only true meaning of "forgiveness," and no one else can do it for me. Dying happens every moment, instantly, as does rebirth, and all it takes is one look in the right direction. The absolute perfection of it is mind-blowing, exploding whatever "mind" I thought I had, and the result is love, blossoming as joy. To think I once called something a problem. To think I actually bought into the idea that "Life is difficult, and then you die," a belief I held so close to my heart for so long, and all the drinking and carousing and crimes I committed during those years, especially after my LSD blowouts in the '60s, perhaps to keep from disappearing. Were they problems created unbeknownst to me, that I might back myself into a corner so tight I had no choice but to find the truth? Who, or What, created this story, only to discover Itself? Who else is there?

"Whatever happens, happens to you by you, through you; you are the creator, enjoyer and destroyer of all you perceive."
—*Sri Nisargadatta Maharaj*

TRIKE

"God is alive, and magic is afoot!"
—Buffy Saint Marie

A friend offered me his bike to ride. Since I hadn't been on a bike in over 40 years, he suggested I first try it out on the lawn in his back yard. Because of arthritis and double hip replacements, I couldn't get my leg over the seat or the crossbar, so I mounted from a porch step. The ride lasted no more than 30 feet, most of it while tilting precariously out of control and bound for the rocks surrounding the garden. I'd say the first thing that hit the ground was my head, but from my perspective I don't have one, although at that moment I had to wonder. There was no pain, only surprise, along with a ringing sensation as if a bell had been struck.

So with the help of a monetary gift, I bought a trike, an adult three-wheeler with a large basket between the rear wheels. Rather than walk with a cane, I could now ride. Everything became mobile, and no longer was there a need to depend on friends or local buses for markets, doctors' offices, book stores, the library and town hall—everything arrived with the breeze as these upside-down, truncated legs pedaled, right here in this No-thing.

This now has become a meditation. Riding, I am still, watching the trees and bushes and lawns clip by and disappear into this vast Aware Space. There are dozens of bike paths in this city, paved trails winding through wonderlands of greenery, many of them following streams that meander eastward past ponds and lakes populated with ducks and geese. Motorized traffic is forbidden on

105

these trails, and that includes the increasingly popular (and expensive) electric bikes. "Why would anyone buy a motorized bike?" I recently asked a friend. "Why simply coast and miss out on all that good exercise?"

But I must admit there are times I wish I had one, especially when my legs scream with exhaustion climbing the hills at the far end of the countless underpasses built strictly for these trails, underpasses sometimes quickly followed by an overpass. One path follows a freeway some 40 miles, a marathon ride for old geezers like me, but it's on my bucket list anyway, and someday, I swear, I'll watch every mile of it pass this way into the One Space of Experience, right here in this stillness that cannot tire.

And of course, while riding my trike I am acutely aware that magic is "afoot." I've no doubt that God is alive because I see what He sees through this great Eye of His and feel his presence in my own presence. And oh, the magic! Total stillness here—forever still—while the world rushes past and disappears. I watch the scenery shuffle by, the near objects passing quickly and far objects more slowly. Buildings grow and turn and pass, while the ribbon-like path on which the bicycle rides, while appearing narrow at a distance, perfectly widens to accommodate me before vanishing into God's Infinite Eye. And everything happens here, inside. And here's the kicker—everything that happens here IS this Infinite Eye, manifesting as a world of endless and varied movement. Truly, "magic is afoot," and anyone can plainly see the same if only they will look in the right direction and drop the beliefs they learned from others, even if only for a moment, and experience the world as it is presented. No wonder Douglas Harding so often said: Come to your senses! Take what you see on present evidence only.

Doing so, seeing Who I Really Am as the One Awareness or the Eye of God, I realize that distance is learned. As a baby, everything was presented in this Space of Awareness, such as my hand or a toy or my mother's face, along with sounds and tastes and feelings. As I grew older I learned from others the concepts of space and time, and distance became the explanation for separation, not only between two objects but between the acquired concept of who I was in relation to "others," or "me" and who was "not me." These concepts became ingrained over a period of time, thanks to my parents and friends and society (according to what they saw from "over there", which to them was a separate person with a particular name and appearance). So by the time I was ten or eleven years old, I had absorbed an elaborate lie, albeit one that is necessary for socialization, but still a lie. This is the Original Sin, the sin of separation from Who You Really Are, and the cause of countless confrontations and emotional pain. And all the while there is a radical but simple solution: Point at where you thought you had a head and notice that in its place there is nothing but space, space so vast and capacious that anything and everything will easily fit inside, a space that is wide awake and unquestionably lit with a sense of presence, of I-am-ness. The directive is to look, actually drop what you are doing and drop the thoughts and beliefs you have learned from others—and take what you SEE, take exactly what is presented, and in performing that one act, simple and childish though it may seem, there is the return to Truth, the union, or reunion, with God — as God.

Indeed, magic is afoot. Try it. Look back at what you are looking out while walking or jogging.

Or ride a bike. There's magic everywhere!

THE MAN IN THE OTHER BATHROOM

Oh! There you are! Jeez, you just wake up? You look awful!

Thanks. I just said the same about you.

Yes, I suppose you did. From over there, that is.

Here or there, what's the difference? You're looking in a mirror!

Yes, but you see, you're over there. You, as the mirror image, are not here. You're there, in that other bathroom.

Wait a minute! If I'm a reflection, how can I be different than you?

You're not only different, you're the opposite! From here, when I look back at where I once thought I had a face, I see that I am perfectly clear. In fact, so clear that there's nothing here but empty space, lit with awareness—and I'm not saying that awareness is a thing.... Put it this way, what I see here in place of a face is a sort of awake nothing, an awake capacity for the scene, and right now the scene includes this wall and sink and mirror, and of course, the sink and wall and you in that other bathroom over there.

Well I don't see anything of the kind.

Of course not, you're an image, a thing, an object in this awareness that I am. You have no separate existence. Your "life" is this appearance here in awareness.

You could say that about everything, and everyone as well! That sounds like a bad case of solipsism, if you ask me.

On the contrary. It's a *good* case of solipsism, the kind that envelopes everything and everyone in the love of pure awareness. It's the all-inclusive solipsism of God, as opposed to the radical self-centered and exclusionary solipsism of one who believes he or she is a separate individual and all others are objects to be used for self-aggrandizement.

Say what you will, it's blasphemous to compare yourself to God, or worse, to call yourself God.

What else could God be but this open, capacious, undying awareness? The real blasphemy is the belief that one is a separate person, and one who happens to be very much in charge. One who thinks he or she calls all the shots.

So how else am I different?

For one thing, I noticed that you never blink. And of course, you're facing the opposite way, not to mention that you have a face and I don't. You're also turned inside-out, and you're considerably smaller. If I measure you with a ruler at arms' length, you're less than a foot tall! I, on the other hand, have no borders or boundaries, and am so vast that absolutely everything fits within me, within awareness. I am infinite, and can say with confidence that I am capacity for the universe.

What about other people's awareness? How do you juggle that? I want to hear this!

I've never seen another awareness, especially another awareness in another place, as if that were even possible. Search the world over, another awareness will never be found. Remember, awareness is not a thing. It doesn't conform to space/time parameters. It's what space/time happens in. It's infinite because there isn't another awareness to compare it to. It's singular for the same reason. And even "infinite" and "singular" are conditional descriptions in that they cannot apply to that which is prior to conditions and descriptions. Conditions and descriptions apply to things, and again, awareness is not a thing. It's empty and formless, but awake. That's the best I can describe it. Or leave the "I" out of it, and let's say that that's the best it can describe itself.

For me, that's no description at all. It's gobbledygook.

Yes, well, welcome to the world. You and all but a very few have no desire to lose your beliefs. If you did, you'd lose the very world you think you're in. In fact, forgetting Who you really are and what you're really like is the only way to have a world to begin with. It's the Great Game, totally necessary in order to have a "personal history," a "life," even though Who you really are — pure awareness — has no personal history, was never born and can never die.

How do you figure? Countless people are born and countless die every day. You have to be blind not to see that!

I see that there. You, for instance, were born nearly 80 years ago, and will likely die in the near future. But what I see here is entirely different. Here, I see absolutely nothing, no-thing at all. Here, exactly where I am, there is nothing that can die. Only things — objects in space/time, and no doubt space time itself — arise and pass away, some in nanoseconds, others in billions of years. And as I've said, awareness — "awakeness" — is not a thing. Neither is "presence." These terms cannot be objectively defined, but they are obvious when subjectively seen.

So look back at what you are looking out of. Do any of the pointing exercises (see my book The Light That I Am, or any of Richard Lang's wonderful books, or visit The Headless Way website), and have a look, not a think.

But what about these other people you mention? What about all the objects, the things of this world? Or the world itself? You're saying that you're the only one who isn't like this? The only one who isn't material, who isn't mortal?

That's what I'm saying.

Okay. So basically, all beings – humans to amoeba – are like me, and all things, every scene that passes through your awareness, is like me, an object.

Not *my* awareness. Just awareness. There's no one here, so there's no one to claim it. It's not a personal quality that I or anyone else was born with or somehow magically began to radiate from the brain when a certain neuronal complexity arrived during fetal development or after birth. It has no qualities, comes from nowhere, and never ends because everywhere and everywhen is within it. It's spaceless and timeless. It has always been and always will be, always HERE/NOW. And yes, all objects are like you, an object, passing through. It's why I love you.

You love me? Me, the object that you once said "follows you around a lot" – how could you love an object, even if I'm so familiar?

For two reasons: First, you, like all objects in the empty awareness that I am, are inside me. In other words, you are so profoundly a part of me that you and all objects and the world itself are all I can say I am in manifestation. You are what awareness is in manifestation. I manifest as the scene – and right now it happens to be you standing in that other bathroom staring at me. So how could I not love you? You're inside me! I am you, all I can be at this moment, and this moment is all there is!

The other reason is the opposite, and just as important. I love you because you show me what I'm not! I am not a thing, an object. I am not what I look like over there. I am what I look like to myself, right here, when I actually look. You are what I was told I was by others, beginning with my parents, my close relatives, my friends, my school, and just about everyone else right up to this day. You are what for so many years I believed I was, which was a lie. Like practically everyone else, I was hoodwinked as a child. But now I see – actually see – that I'm not like that, not like you. Not here where I am. Thus, you are more than valuable to me. You do me the great service of pointing out, and repeatedly, Who I really am by displaying who I'm not. Oddly, you are the bearer of truth, my salvation, the gift I can never do without. For this, I love you.

Wow! You made me smile!

Yes, I feel that here.

So then I'm okay. All the things I've done in this world, good and bad, and surely the bad outweighs the good, have been for this. To show you Who you are and who you're not, which when you come down to it, are essentially the same.

Yes.

So I'm saved also, along with you?

Yes, absolutely. You become me. You are my teacher, as is everyone and everything else, and at the instant of recognition as to Who I really am, you also become what I am. Actually, you were always that. You were never an object, a separate entity in a vast and implacable universe. You just thought you were. I am you. You are what I am, and you were never anything else.

Jesus the savior, dying to self and thus saving all from sin.

Exactly. Dying to ego-self and becoming Who he really was, thus saving the world. It's the same in Buddhism. When the Buddha became enlightened, all beings were said to be enlightened. The reason, of course, is that there are no other beings, no separate selves, nothing that intrinsically exists outside of empty awareness. Jesus and Buddha and many others recognized this. It's all within, all internal. The universe is an appearance in awareness. Some therefore say it's not real. But it is. Everything that appears in awareness is the only "reality" there is. It's just not where we think it is, nor what we think it is. It's not "out there," as in "I'm here inside my body and the universe is "out there," and I exist as an individual in it." On the contrary, the universe is a manifestation of awareness, always appearing right here, in awareness. The two are never separate because they are the same—awareness, and that which it is aware of. And since you mentioned Jesus, it might be helpful to remember that the real meaning of "sin" is "separation from God." Or as I would say, existing apart from empty awareness, from Who I really am.

Okay. But soon I need to get ready for my day. Disguised as you, of course. Maybe I should brush my teeth. I'd say that you should brush yours too, but I know what you'll say.

Like, "What teeth?" Yes, I see you and others cleaning their teeth, but from my point of view, I bring the brush forward and it disappears into this aware space, and suddenly there is the taste of mint.

Sounds nutty, even childish, doesn't it?

Yes, to anyone relying on their intellect. But awakening has nothing to do with intellect. Relying on one's senses is the way in. Remember, it was Jesus who said, "Truly I tell you, unless you change and become like little children, you will never enter the kingdom of heaven." (Matthew 18:2-6). The point is, you are already awake, you have simply forgotten. So yes, it sounds childish, but children, particularly babies, haven't yet been told that they are what they look like from someone else's perspective, someone like their mother. But mother is not where baby is. Mother is where she is, and because she believes she is a separate self-existing entity and she sees her baby as "over there," she conveys to her baby that this is what her baby is also, a separate entity. Babies know nothing of the sort. All there is from a babies' perspective is pure openness, filled with all manner of fleeting objects—rattles, nipples, the ceiling, mother's face, and so on. Babies are already awake, the natural state, though they don't know it. So yes, as you said, it sounds childish, and for good reason.

It's backwards from the way we normally think.

Is it ever! Seeing Who you really are is an exercise in being backwards and upside-down. Try as I might to beat that for fun and enjoyment, I can't. It's hilarious, because my previous belief was so at odds with the natural way. Actually, Who I really am is not the backward state; the truly backward state is the idea that we are all separate individuals self-existing in these body/minds referred to by such and such name and each having certain qualities and characteristics. It's a joke. I am not my body/mind. In fact, it's the Great Joke mentioned by the Ch'an masters of ancient China.

You are always at rest. You never move, do you, even when you are doing everyday things like shaving and washing your face and walking to the store or riding your bike to a doctor's appointment?

That's right. I shave your face, not mine. I have no face. I am this singular and awake and enormous Eye, and everything, including these hands and torso and legs and whatever sensations are present during shaving are, like all objects, part of the scene, as is the floor and wall and mirror and you standing there staring at me in that other bathroom. And by the way, I say that this Eye, this awake space, is singular because I have never seen—actually seen—another Eye, another aware space, and even if I had, it would be inside this awake Eye that I am, and would thus be an object. And I say it's enormous because everything fits within it. It takes in, or is capacity for, the entire universe, including all the passing thoughts and beliefs that are attached to whatever objects appear in it. This Eye, which some have referred to as the Eye of God, is not subject to measurement because there isn't another Eye to compare it to. So looking back at what I am looking out of, I see this great awake nothing, this empty Eye filled with the scene, and I see no dividing line between this empty Eye and the scene. They are the same. Nothing/everything (void/form) is one view, and that singular view cannot include another empty Eye. It's singular, non-dual. There cannot be any sort of duality anywhere, any separation between a scene and that which is aware of the scene. They are one. And truly, calling the view "singular" or "one" is misleading because it implies that there is a second somewhere, when actually there isn't even a "one." It is probably best referred to as "Suchness" or "I-I" or any term that implies a lack of objectivity. I often use the term "Pure Subjectivity" to represent what cannot be described.

And getting back to your question of movement, Who I really am is at rest in every situation, no matter what. Both Douglas Harding and Richard Lang have cited the examples of flying in a plane to a distant destination, which is the conventional manner of describing a trip. Actually, as they have pointed out, the destination arrives to this aware space, this Eye, which never moves an inch. So of course, Who you really are is always rested, wide awake. This is true of walking, jogging, riding a bike or driving a car. Who you really are never left, never went anywhere, and everything conveniently arrived right where you have always been, which is Here. How's that for relaxation?

Yes, and it doesn't apply to me, does it?

Not over there, no. Not unless you come here, turn around, and become Who you really are, in which case you are "I." Over there, as in the case of all "over theres," you are an object in this awake and capacious Eye ("I").

So all I need to do is turn around and become Who you really are. I'm going to do that now, and oddly, I'll see you, or your body, walk out of the bathroom. From your vantage point, that is. Or, at that point, as Who you (I) really am!

Well said. Let's go.

WHERE'S THE REMOTE?

"The foolish reject what they see and not what they think; the wise
reject what they think and not what they see."
—Ch'an Master Huang-Po Hsi-yun' (d. 850)

God's world is vertical because nothing is remote. Everything, every arriving and passing scene is experienced "Here," in (and as) awareness. This is why there is no "remote." This is why God is omnipresent.

And consider: There is no fixed size. Objects grow and shrink depending on how they appear Here where they are experienced. For instance, a woman or a man "at a distance" appears as a tiny figure: say, the size of one of those toys on the set of a model railroad layout. That man or woman at a distance is not actually 5'8" tall, as one might assume. Not Here, where they appear. In reality they are tiny, less than an inch tall!

You say, "Yes, but let's use the example of a chair. I can measure the chair with a ruler and prove it is 3 feet tall, and I know that even though the chair is across the room, it is still 3 feet tall."

And I say, believing myself to be an object separate from and surrounded by a world of separate objects, such a claim may appear to be true. But the premise is wrong. I am not an object existing in a world of objects. I am Subject, and everything that appears does so Here where it is actually experienced, and Here, the manner in which everything is experienced is exactly as it is experienced. Using the senses, going on present evidence only and not relying on erroneous thoughts and beliefs that I learned from others, I see this. And I take what I see, not what others say I should see. That chair is tiny, as is the ruler you left next to it, so I am relying on what I see Here, not what I think "over there."

For instance, suppose I walk in front of a full-length mirror. Walking toward the mirror, I am watching a miniature but growing version of "J.C." approaching. I have learned from others that that image in the mirror is "me." However, here where I am, I see that Who I Really Am—pure, empty awareness—is motionless (being no-thing, there is nothing that could move). And seeing Who I Really Am, I see the person in the mirror (and the mirror itself) growing. Nothing really happens "out there." No one actually approaches. The person-image grows larger and, thinking conventionally, I assume "I'm approaching." Conversely, the image grows smaller, and I assume "I'm retreating." But as pure empty awareness, these assumptions are nonsense. They are no more than an exercise in illusory assumptions. Growing and shrinking appear Here within empty awareness, not "out there." There is no "out there." There never was and never will be. Everything happens Here inside the oneness of awareness, which is Who I Really Am, and anyone can say the same, knowing there is no one else!

Last week, while shuffling through the papers and the pillows on the living room couch, my housemate said to me, "Have you seen the remote?"

I had to admit I hadn't.

THE TUNNEL OF TRUTH

"What is the meaning of direct perception? Perception that sees only itself. No other."
—*Ramana Maharshi*

I rent a bedroom in this old house. Across the hall from my bedroom is a closet, and on the inside of the closet door is a full-sized mirror. When the door is open and I step into the hallway and see the image in the mirror—the person others call J.C.—I am nearly always startled. For 35 years all I had, all that any inmate could buy from our prison canteen, was a shaving mirror not much bigger than my hand. Now I am confronted by the full-sized appearance of a balding and bow-legged old man standing behind a sheet of glass staring back at me, truly a snapshot of impending doom if ever there was one.

As him, I'm a goner. As him, I'm about to walk the "Green Mile." As him, death may be a gift to others.

But thank God I'm not him. Thank God, right here, I look nothing like him. Here, I am Clear Space, pure capacity for what appears, which happens to be a full-sized version of the scofflaw I've too often referred to as "me." Looking down at his right-side-up body there and then at my headless and upside-down body here, I am grateful beyond words. I am, as they say, all smiles, and he responds by smiling back. The thought appears that this immediate situation is uproariously hilarious, that, had things not worked out exactly as they had, I could easily believe that I am that passing and decaying image with so little time left on this planet—what a joke!

For only things die, and here, where I am, there is no thing, but a no-thing that is wide awake, and awake to Itself as no thing. Over there—the image of a thing called a human being, one that is on its way out, bound for the eventual graveyard that awaits all things.

But this isn't all. Observing Awake Emptiness is only half the story; a step, let's say, in the right direction. Because not only am I this empty and aware Eye that takes in and is the foundation of the universe, I am also that which is taken in! I am both void and form simultaneously, which is to say, unless I see I am no-thing, I cannot see I am everything. Ultimately, it takes both to be none. To cite the title of one of Wei Wu Wei's books, "All Else Is Bondage."

To clearly experience this, cut both ends off a paper bag and place one end against a bathroom mirror and your face in the other end, then tell the truth. Not something you believe to be true because you learned it from others in the past, but what you presently see! When I do this, I see no face at this end. Yet this end is my end. What I see here at this end is void, fully aware and fully present, while what I see at that end is what others see and what cameras record, from that distance. But at this end, nothing. Only Presence. A wholly different sense of I AM.

And to complete this Vision that ends all visions, upon seeing Empty Awareness at this end, I also see the scene appearing within it, which happens to be the face at that end. This occurs simultaneously, but it is crucial that Empty Awareness at this end not be overlooked. This way, our usual habitual attachment to the scene (and only the scene) is then transformed into Oneness, or to use a better term, "Within-ness." Void becomes Capacity for the scene, form. The two are seen as One, inside. So completely inside, in fact, that the distinction between "inside" and "outside" are no longer relevant. Nor is there any need for the term "One," which is understood to have functioned as merely provisional.

To quote Rabbi Rami Shapiro, "This is what is meant by 'God is one.' Not that God is singular rather than plural; but that there is only one reality and that reality is God." God being Pure Subjectivity, both seer and seen.

And note the words of Ch'an master Huang-Po: "A perception, sudden as blinking, that subject and object are one, will lead to a deeply mysterious understanding, and by this understanding you will awaken to the truth."

There is another interesting feature of the paper bag experiment: The term "timelessness," which cannot truly be understood, can at least be seen. Empty Awareness, that which I've called "Pure Subjectivity" or "Awareness/Presence," and what I've referred to in another of my books as "The Unfigureoutable" (a word I borrowed from the author David Lang), is recognized as prior to understanding, prior to description, and prior to space and time because there is absolutely nothing tangible here, nothing that can be touched, measured, or changed in any way, and it is only things—objects—that are subject to space and time. In the paper bag, my end is "empty" because there is nothing objective here. Objects are "out there" at the other end of the tunnel. At my end: the Unfigureoutable—aware, conscious, present, yet no thing, and therefore timeless. At the other end: the image of that old guy's face, appearing as a thing, and therefore subject to space and time. In this sense, the tunnel acts as a bridge between timelessness and time, no-thing at my end and some-thing at that end, both of which can be seen. And as a Seeing friend once pointed out, the paper bag thus functions as a time machine.

For instance, no matter how close an object is, there is still a fraction of a second before I experience it. Light from Alpha Centauri takes 4.367 light years to reach me, and I then "see" it. Light from my nose blur (actually there are two, one on the left and one on the right) takes, say, a microsecond for me to register it. But here, where I actually do experience it, no time passes because: 1) there is no object to be registered, and 2) Awareness is what is doing the registering!

And for those reasons, obviously there can be nothing prior to Awareness. Therefore Awareness, where experience occurs, cannot be anything in space/time, whereas any point along the shopping bag wall will appear to reflect a different time. As Douglas Harding explained, that which is incoming is reduced to nothing; that which is outgoing is produced from nothing. But both are experienced here where I AM.

Thus, in what might be called the Self-manifestation of Awareness, time proceeds from timelessness at this end of the bag to the time-full scene "out there." Likewise, all that appears proceeds from this space-less point of Awareness here to dimensions of space "out there." This is why Awareness is said to be the foundation of all things, the creator of the universe, God Herself.

So find a paper shopping bag, cut both ends off, and find a mirror—or better yet, ask a friend to place their face in the opposite end. Then drop beliefs and take exactly what you presently see. Consider that you just might be answering the ultimate questions so many have never answered, such as what you are and what this universe is, and doing so with that cheapest but most significant of all forms of scientific equipment, the paper bag. Call it five-cent enlightenment.

Who said God doesn't have a great sense of humor?

INFINITELY SILLY

The terms "Infinite Universe" and "No Space/time" are essentially the same. Here—an infinitesimal no-point which is prior to quarks, prior to space/time, prior to thought; and at the farthest fringes of the universe—matter rushing headlong toward the speed of light where space is solid and time stops. So in a sense, infinity happens Here where there is no-thing, and infinity happens Out There where there is everything! Both are prior to existence, and in between, there appears a universe, and this is What You Are.

And of course, the idea that you are Infinite suggests a total lack of boundaries, as does no-space and no-time (timelessness). Opening to this possibility, we might suffer a sense of meaninglessness and loss of control, our self-importance as individuals. And this is what we fear the most—the loss of self—the irony being that we never had one to begin with!

Of course, those of us who want to remain as "us" have a way of putting a cap, or limit, on the infinite. If we believe in God in the usual sense that popular religions posit, we have a comforting parental figure (even as a spirit) who neatly provides us with an address in a familiar body and mind we call home— which of course turns out to be a cul-de-sac that repeatedly returns us to our customary notions of reality and the usual confrontations of day-to-day life, tragic though they may be.

But to Christian and Jewish mystics and Sufi masters, the terms God or Yahweh or The Friend refer to an altogether different figure, one that is not a "figure" at all but an unnamable Source at the core of all being. Knowing this God is knowing Who one truly is; it is the recognition that God is a Oneness that knows no "one," never mind the absurdity of "two." This God is Who You Really Are, disguised as who you think you are. This God is Unmanifested Awareness manifesting as anything and everything.

But in case you think this God is impersonal, He couldn't be more personal. After all, He is Who You Are. How much more personal could He be? How much more intimate?

And in case you think this God is grim, the truth is that She is the epitome of irony, not to mention comedy. In fact, She's a riot, the cause of endless laughter. Here She is, right where you are and in plain view, so close you miss Her—and there you are, out building monumental structures in an attempt to reach Her, spire upon spire stabbing the heavens so She'll notice you. What foolishness She inspires!

And in case you think this God is closed for business, He couldn't be more open and available. She is the open secret, the gateless gate, the timeless Now and space-less Here, the sum of which is NOWHERE, right where you are.

And in case you think you have a choice to reject this God and remain a separate "you," come to your senses (literally!) and See that it isn't "you" playing that part to begin with! You can't even have that! There is no way out of being Who You Really Are, and even who you think you are isn't you thinking it! So why not be Who You Really Are? After all, you cannot not be.

And just in case you're still hanging onto that thread of separate self by supposing you'll awaken somewhere else or at some other time, point at the Space above your shoulders and notice that there is no way out of this no-place where You are, for all places are within You. And as for some other time, See that in your Absence and Stillness there is nothing that could register time. To quote D.E. Harding: "This moment is timeless, and there's no way out of this moment."

Isn't it marvelous that we can be so infinitely silly? Isn't it wonderful that God—Who You Really Are—has come up with these joys and tragedies and, right here and right now, this return to ItSelf? How simply amazing to be all this and nothing at all!

VACATION

The root word of "vacation" is the Latin vacare: "to be empty, free, or at leisure," or having the meaning of "a state of being unoccupied."

One aspect of awakening to Who You Really Are is the recognition that, underlying all the surrounding hubbub of your life, you are always and permanently on vacation. Recently this was brought home to me when I went on three short trips, one of which was a three-day excursion into the Rocky Mountains with a friend who, for that short time, was temporarily in "a state of being unoccupied" by his pressing responsibilities.

We visited old haunts where we once had lived or worked. On the first day we cruised the towns where my friend, a successful businessman in the past, formerly had accounts in the restaurant trade, places that were now mostly unrecognizable. The second day, we drove forty miles on a gravel road to a mountain town in which the house I once rented was currently painted a scandalous pink and the old theater I ran on weekends was now a combination bar and antique shop, devoid of customers. The third day, we drove home, wishing the trip had been longer and planning for our next, maybe to the Midwest and East Coast where our childhood memories lie.

Overall, I have to say, we traveled highways that were once country roads and searched for others we could not find on a map, not, perhaps, because they were no longer there but because there were no maps we could find—at least not the kind we were familiar with that could once be purchased at any gas station along the way. And of course, we found rooms we had reserved in the usual motels, one even with an indoor pool where we discovered we could now sink a lot easier than we could swim. And strangely, other than at the remote campsite where we stopped for a packed sandwich, the highlight of the trip was a return to a Bavarian eatery that currently served Mexican food, *huevos rancheros* done the way they can only be done south of the border: homemade corn tortillas, perfectly fried eggs, and fresh salsa picante.

In the past, outside of summer breaks between school years and the week or two surrounding major holidays, I don't remember ever having taken a vacation. At least not during the period of my life after college when I held a real job, brief though that was. As a criminal, some might say that I was on vacation all the time, but that wasn't the case — in many ways I was busier than I ever was, and the stress was at times unbearable. And those decades in prison? No vacation, I can guarantee.

But then I discovered the real vacation, not one that I take but the one that I am. The first of the three recent trips was, perhaps, the standard variety vacation, filled with the continuous distraction of interesting sights and good conversation with my friend. A great time, to be sure.

But the second and third trips were another matter. They may have started off the same, distractions galore, but they soon became what I call the real sightseeing (or Sight-seeing!), an entirely different manner of attending to the facts.

The second trip was a one-day affair in which two friends and I boarded an old narrow-gauge mining train pulled by an ancient locomotive. At first, I was mostly conscious of the trees passing by close to the track, one after the other growing and turning as they approached, the scent of pine carried along by the breeze. But then the vision opened to take in not only the scene but that in which the scene appeared, and each tree became my personal invitation to follow it home, to see the place, or was it the no-place?, where each disappeared into this Empty Awareness that I am. The engine chugged up the mountain and the open-air cars followed, and it occurred to me that, along with the cars, the train was towing what was left of this "me" while I, wide open and clearly gone, simultaneously created and witnessed this miraculous spectacle out of nothing-at-all, pure Awareness manifesting as trees and rocks and mountain and sky, and, winding up the narrowing track, this puffing relic of the1800's.

And the third trip? Two weeks passed, and summer was rapidly turning to fall when a call came from a friend whom I'd told about a farfetched entry on my "wish list," which, given my age, I think I said was a "bucket list." To my surprise, he said he'd be at the house with his truck on the very next weekend, and would take my housemate and me on a half day's journey up to a high mountain pass at tree line for a bike ride down to the bottom, 14 miles of wild hairpin turns on a narrow path, a steep coast all the way with plenty of serious braking. The thought of the bike ride was thrilling, of course, an adventure I wanted to experience for certain. But it also took me to the edge, to a place where fear can rule and even ruin the day, and I've no doubt that others have felt the same. I rode a two-wheeler instead of my trike for this trip, and for a moment at the top just before we began our descent, I hesitated, visions of one possible accident after another flashing before me, each with the worst of possible outcomes.

"What nonsense," I remember saying aloud, and following my pal, I pushed off into oblivion and plunged into the void, each mile rushing by and into this Awake Space of no accidents, no injuries, no death at all.

For what is there to die? What do I see when I look within, here where I am? I see absolutely nothing! Only "things" — objects—can suffer death, and I am obviously no-thing. This Aware Emptiness is birth-less and deathless, no-where and no-when. I am not the self-existent separate individual I may look like to others, not what I learned as a child and have believed for so long. This body-mind named J.C. has never held the central position. He is an object, one of the countless "ten thousand things" appearing moment by moment, while I—Pure Presence/Awareness—have never been a thing, nor anything at all.

It was over, as they say, "in no time at all." We sped from the top of the pass down through golden stands of aspens, raced under and across bridges and past fields of wildflowers, then out and across an empty ski town to a narrow canyon where the path eased for a moment, then sharply dropped again to follow a whitewater creek for the final miles. At the end, across a wooden bridge, our friend was waiting with his truck, and the day ended like the incredible path, abruptly and with a grin.

Riding "shotgun" on the way home in the truck, now with this Empty Awareness like a glassless windshield into which the highway endlessly vanished, I kept thinking: Are we not all on vacation, forever "empty, free, and at leisure?" And won't one look in the right direction confirm it?

Perhaps not. But isn't it worth the look? And if, being no-thing, we discover there really is a state we could be in, wouldn't it surely be "a state of being unoccupied?"

TAKING IT TO THE STREETS

"The way to do is to be."
—Lao Tzu

A few months after I was released when I was musing over what to do, a psychologist friend said to me, "Be your gift."

What gift? I thought. Writing? Was this what he meant?

I pondered this question, despite the fact that I already knew the answer and knew that it would again arrive with a laugh from that place prior to thought. Writing, or anything else I could do, whether or not I could do it well, wasn't my gift. My gift was the gift that all beings of all descriptions have—whether or not they can express it—and it has everything to do with being and only indirectly to do with doing. It is the gift that I and that all beings cannot not have. Or rather, cannot not be. It is the gift that is empty, awake, filled with the scene, and supremely intelligent, clever beyond all we can imagine (after all, it came up with a universe!). The gift is not what I am, but that I am, and this presence, this I-am-ness, although no "thing," is the foundation of all things everywhere, all space and time. In short, it is the "be" in "Be your gift."

This advice from my psychologist friend was, of course, my reminder for the day, the latest in a string of countless reminders since I had first seen the awake emptiness at my core, the pure awareness behind all my so-called "doing."

Which is how it has been for me. Perhaps we all experience truth differently. Few awaken and never return to the misunderstanding of who or what they really are. Others glimpse reality and only return to the realization years later, often conflicted between the ultimate insight and dealing with the complexities of life. Most, of course, live out their span in their private dreams, never recognizing the glory of Who they really are.

Here, the Beatific Vision has never left, although much of the time it awaits in the background, especially during times of distraction. Fortunately—and this is the genius of Douglas Harding and the Headless Way—the Vision is always available, no matter what the mood or circumstance. All that is required is a look, and there you are—lit, awake, present, and empty, so entirely empty that you are capacity for every objective appearance in the world, as well as all the thoughts and feelings attached to those objects. Each look is always the same, even though each appearance may be different. Each look is spaceless and timeless and filled to the brim with space/time. Therefore, seeing no-thing filled with everything is always identical, no matter what appears within the emptiness that you are. Why? Because void and form are void/form, the same.

Some say that form requires void, but void does not require form, that, for instance, objects require awareness to be aware of them, but awareness does not require objects. As the physicist Amit Goswami put it: "There is no object in space-time without a conscious subject looking at it." When I look here, I see awake nothing, pure awareness. But simultaneously I also see it filled with the scene, whatever that scene may be. Although I may refer to this awake no-thing at my core as pure awareness, I cannot say I have ever seen pure awareness as an object because pure awareness is what is looking! And yet it is here, and although there is nothing to see here, I see this nothing plain as day! Wei Wu Wei used the term "apprehend" rather than "see," but this conscious nothing here where I assumed I had a face is clearly visible, as clearly present, as Harding once said, as seeing the absence of eggs on his morning breakfast plate.

So it is awake, but is no object. It is pure consciousness—boundless and uncontained, while all things are contained within it. It has been termed Subjectivity, or Original Face, which points to the wondrous fact that, while all things are within it, all things within it are it, so that whatever appears within the pure consciousness that you are is what you are. Again, to paraphrase the Buddhist formula:

First there are mountains and rivers (the common view that objects intrinsically exist "out there" in the world apart from the viewer);

Then there are no mountains and rivers (recognizing that you are pure awareness here/now);

Then once again there are mountains and rivers (as what you are.)

To settle the matter as to which comes first—awareness or object—I say to See for yourself. In my experience, they arise together but not as two. And yet I can clearly see the empty and pure awareness here as opposed to the scene that appears within it. Both visions are available, and although it may seem odd when looking from the position of duality, both are one and the same. In the first instance, they can be seen as separate, but in the final and awakened view, they arise together and are not two. Have a look, and see what cannot be explained. You are the authority on Who you are.

So why the reminders? Why should I need them, and what function could they serve? Seeing what—or Who—I see when I look, am I so conditioned to attach to the popular belief of a separate self that I need to be continually reminded of Who I really am? Why can't I simply drop the baggage of the past and board the train of no one going nowhere?

But the delicious irony of this apparent need for reminders is that there is no separate "who" who needs them, and moreover, that reminders arise as part and parcel of truth itself. The whole universe, appearing moment by moment as each passing scene, is my mirror, my teacher, my reminder. The reason is simple. The universe, appearing as whatever scene, is Who I am! I am appearing to myself! I—I who am not—am manifesting as whatever, which is What I am! In fact, if that were otherwise — heaven forbid! —there would be no universe!

Byron Katie once commented that she was the most self-centered person she knew —everything she did was for and about herself. As she put it, "When I say, 'I love you,' there's no personality talking. It's self-love: I'm only talking to myself. The way I experience it is that It is only talking to Itself. If I say, 'Let me pour you some tea,' It is pouring Its own tea for Itself, and the tea is Itself. It's so self-absorbed that It leaves no room for any other. Nothing."

So what to do?

Why, be my gift! What else? What else could I do?

And what else could you do, you who were never "you," who are THIS? What should you do with the remainder of life, however short or long it may appear to be? Why, nothing! There's nothing you should do because as a separate you you're already being done! And being done along with everything else apparently being done, in, by, and as Who you really are. What a crazy notion we've had, this counterfeit "I" supposedly doing all these things, as if that were actually possible. And in case we think we've at least done that, made that mistake called a "crazy notion," no, we can't even have that, for it too is part of the movie that arises in, by, and as the Empty Awareness that we are....

...And yet, what fun it all is! Such a fabulous show, and on such a grand scale! What perfection! And what intelligence! This world, all from Nothing-at-all, and all for Itself! To quote Byron Katie again: "When the 'I' arises, welcome to the movie of who you think you are. Get the popcorn, here it comes! If you investigate, and the 'I' arises, there's no attachment. It's just a great movie."

So I take it to the street, this drama of who I think I am, this character with this part on the stage of this thought called "world." Someone once asked if I felt obligated to teach others Who they really are, which of course is impossible other than to show them how to see for themselves. In my case, after many years of searching, I first saw — actually saw—the undeniable emptiness/presence at my core when I came across Harding's article in a magazine and pointed back at what I was looking out of. I was floored. It was so ridiculously easy, so childishly simple, so "here-all-the-time stupid," that I burst out laughing, the only proper acknowledgment there is to something so absurdly un-religious and at the same time so exquisitely sacred.

But when it comes to sharing the obvious, there are others who are more capable than I am, in particular Richard Lang who was only 17 when he first met Harding and saw the Aware Emptiness at his core. Although Harding introduced tens of thousands to the same, he once said that the only way he could make a difference for others was to See for himself, to attend to Who he really was and to leave the rest to take care of itself.

And I often refer to this when I am struck by the mistaken idea of "obligation-to-others," either as the result of a question from some supposed "other," or from one of my own thoughts passing through. "Where are these 'others?'" I find myself asking, the question itself being the answer. THIS—here and now—is where the movie, the world, and every possible scene, including all that thought labels "other," is where it begins and ends—in and as Empty Awareness, which is Who I really am, and Who you really are. The same.

So be your gift. It's easy. You already are.

THIS JUST SHOULDN'T HAVE HAPPENED

A friend visited today to help me with a issue concerning the future of this book, and during our conversation he mentioned that he had recently read an author who cited Harding's enthusiastic position on why there shouldn't be anything at all. Years ago when I read the same in a number of Harding's books, I had the impression Harding was literally gushing with astonishment that Awareness had seemingly, as he put it, "popped up out of nothing," that there could be — or should be — simply a blank, a zero, the absolute darkness of nothing forever. But the fact that there was Awareness and an entire universe of everything within it — well, that was just incredibly improbable, truly worthy of the highest reverence. It just shouldn't have happened. And the fact that it did, that there is this Presence, this I-Am-Ness, was astounding, moment by miraculous moment!

"Yes, that's the true basis of gratitude," I said to my friend. "Seeing that, I can't help but feel grateful for everything. Literally everything! It's really a stunning insight. It manifests as an unconstrained fountain of Being, all from Awareness, from this Awake No-Thing-At-All."

We talked over coffee at the kitchen table, and I was thankful that he accepted the other half of a pecan pie of which I couldn't possibly eat another slice, and we talked about the crazy state of affairs in Washington politics and how the world is a mirror to our attitudes and actions — and then we talked about looking Here and seeing Who we really are and the difference it makes in our attitudes and actions and how easily that issues forth in reciting gratitudes and intentions (he is a member of Intenders For The

Highest Good), and finally about this book and his music and how we pass forward gifts that turn out to be to our Self. And how, in the end, and at the "gateless gate," there's nothing more that can be said.

And when he was leaving, at the door, I hugged him like a brother and thanked him, then watched him walk to his car. In the momentary silence that followed, I thanked him again, then thanked the world for this communion of self and other as Self, and for this day, a day truly worthy of the highest reverence.

Like every day.

Love is so vast within itself.
It's so vast that it will burn you up.
It's so jealous and greedy for itself mirrored back that it will leave you nothing.
And when you're feeling that if you don't give it away you'll die in it, it's so vast that there's nothing you can do with it.
All you can do is be it."

—Byron Katie

ACKNOWLEDGEMENTS

Profound thanks to Jan Hamer for your friendship and encouragement over the years. Likewise to Richard Lang, whose clear SEEING has meant more than I can say. Thanks to Oscar Senn for his painting "Shadow Walking," and to Charlie for his tech savvy in getting this book to print. Thanks also to Aleta for your support and for backing me in this project. Thank you Fr. Bob for always being there (right Here), and thanks to Rich for heading me in the right direction. Nicole, and Wayne—how could I ever thank you enough for this freedom? Thank you Gary, Tom, Craig, Woody, Joe. And always, never last nor least, my profound thanks to my dear friend Walter.

For more information about Douglas Harding and several simple but effective "experiments" confirming Who You Really Are, please see The Headless Way website at www/headless.org

ABOUT THE AUTHOR

J.C. Amberchele was born in Philadelphia in 1940, attended a Quaker school, then colleges in Pennsylvania and New York, earning a B.A. in psychology. He first became interested in the nature of the Self in the 1960s when he took LSD, but didn't become deeply involved in spiritual matters until after he went to prison several decades later. During that time he studied the works of Wei Wu Wei, Ramana Maharshi, Nisargadatta Maharaj, Byron Katie, and many others, until happening upon an article by Douglas Harding that allowed him to actually see Who he really was. Since then, he has been practicing Seeing, and is the author of four previous books on the subject published by Non-Duality Press. He was incarcerated for two years in a Mexican prison, and for 35 years in the U.S.

Made in the USA
Lexington, KY
12 January 2019